joy No Matter What

P9-CDU-163

joy *No Matter What*

Make **3** Simple Choices to Access Your Inner Joy

Carolyn Hobbs

CONARI PRESS

First published in 2005 by Conari Press,
an imprint of Red Wheel/Weiser, LLC
York Beach, ME

With offices at:
368 Congress Street
Boston, MA 02210
www.redwheelweiser.com

LIBRARY OF CONGRESS CATALOGING-IN-PUBLICATION DATA
Hobbs, Carolyn.
 Joy, no matter what : make three simple choices to access your inner joy / Carolyn Hobbs.
  p. cm.
Includes bibliographical references.
ISBN 1-57324-968-8
1. Joy. I. Title.
BF575.H27H63 2005
152.4'2—dc22   2004023254

Book design by Maxine Ressler
Typeset in Minion, ITC Kallos, and ITC Bailey Sans

Printed in Canada

TCP

12 11 10 09 08 07 06 05

8   7   6   5   4   3   2   1

To Jo Alexander,
whose wise, loving compassion and generous wisdom
has been invaluable in writing this book and in
finding my own joy.

To my mother,
whose own pain and suffering first opened my eyes
and heart to the path of consciousness.

Contents

Acknowledgments

I am deeply grateful to Caroline Pincus, book midwife, whose confidence, strength, and gifted editing skills formed a pillar of support in writing and publishing this book. She generously offered help, encouragement, and countless networking ideas at every juncture, including introducing this book idea to Jan Johnson, my publisher. I also thank my literary agent, Susan Schulman, for always believing in my writing. Her reassurance, respect, and sharp business sense helped us find exactly the right publisher. My editors, Kate Hartke and Jill Rogers, have been invaluable in polishing this manuscript into its final form.

I am eternally indebted to my spiritual family of friends, whose personal lifelong commitments to living in Essence help me every day to find the courage and strength to live in my essential Being. First, I feel deeply grateful to my beloved sister in spirit and in life, Jo Alexander, whose unconditional love, Universal wisdom, and compassionate support held me in love every day as I wrote this book.

I express deep gratitude to my mentor, spirit sister, and beloved friend, Devi Weisenberg, who constantly said yes to holding my deep pain in her heartfelt compassion and loving crone wisdom. For years, she has witnessed and healed my body, heart, and soul with the rarified love, truth telling, courage, wisdom, gentleness, and grace that can only come from years of devoting her self to Essence. Her reading of this manuscript helped polish the tools for connecting with our Being. I also thank Stan Weisenberg, her husband and my friend, for his lifelong devotion to healing with his hands and heart.

I am forever grateful to my beloved friend and spirit sister, Debra Chamberlin-Taylor, whose fierce passion for helping others wake up in this lifetime inspires me every day. Over the years, she has generously been there for me in joy and in pain—as a beloved friend, spiritual teacher, gifted therapist, and playmate as we walk this path of awakening together. Her lovingkindness meditations, devotion to the deepest truth, wise knowing, and committed love helped me fearlessly show up and write this book. I also thank her husband, and my friend, George Taylor for his humor, compassion, and support.

I am indebted to Pamela Polland and Bill Ernst for graciously open-ing their hearts and their Maui home to me year after year. Pamela's lifelong commitment to joy in her everyday life, and her willingness to openly share painful life stories, inspired my writing. Bill's gentle, caring presence offered a helping hand at every juncture. Their help in overcoming my fear of the ocean transformed into fearlessly writing my truth. And a special thanks to my good women friends Joan Lohman, Carole Wampole, and Janet Jacobs for their ongoing support and encouragement while I wrote this book.

I am grateful to Teresa Von Braun, my friend and Diamond Heart practitioner, who I fondly call "my eyes." Her crystalline clarity and expansive view of reality helped me complete this book on joy at the same time that my mother was dying.

I am indebted to Gay and Kathlyn Hendricks, whose clear trans-mission of the vast wisdom of the body helped me discover the unlim-ited capacity for love and healing in our bodies. They taught me how to presence, set intentions, and honor inner wisdom.

I am ever grateful to my lifelong friend, Eleanor Greenlee, who opened the doors of consciousness to me and first helped me touch my aliveness. As my Bioenergetics therapist, she introduced Wilhelm Reich, Al Lowen, Carl Jung, and others to me. As my friend she has loved me unconditionally.

The following teachers have impacted my work and my life in count-less ways: Marion Woodman, thank you for embodying the voice of the conscious feminine and bringing her wisdom to our awareness. Jack Kornfield, Pema Chodron, and Tarthang Tulku, thank you for devoting your lives to Westernizing Buddhism and making it so acces-sible to Americans. Pat Rodegast and Judith Stanton, thank you for channeling the wisdom of one of my favorite teachers, Emmanuel. Julia Cameron, thank you for inviting me, and all writers, to keep show-ing up and write what wants to be written. And I thank Mother Nature, whose eternal silence and loving acceptance nurtures me every day.

It Is Not Just The Words

It is not just the words we speak.
It is the bull elk at full run,
under the moon
that is heard
in the voice itself.

It is the sight of the salmon
straining to swim home,
a quivering silver flash

that melts us down,
renders us back to the breath
and beyond.

—DEVI WEISENBERG

Expanding into Everyday Joy

M ost of us think of joy as something we have to create or seek out. We believe it's only the special people or activities in our lives that bring us a sense of joy. I do it, too. For instance, I just returned from a two-hour hike on one of those warm, sunny, late September mornings that I love about southwest Colorado. The cloudless sky is that deep turquoise blue that I can lose myself in for hours. I feel filled with a sense of joy.

I also find joy in the silence of nature. I love seeing the baby fawn tracks carved in the dirt right next to the not-so-tiny mama deer tracks on the narrow animal trail we share. I smile inside while watching a red-tailed hawk circle overhead, hunting for lunch. Today, I even saw black bear tracks crossing the fire road, which is rare. In November, when the elk return from their summer cavorting above the tree line, I'll breathe deep and fill my nostrils with their wild, musky scent. On special mornings, I get to peek at the whole herd of forty-some elk grazing before winter snows bury their food. I love this wild place.

I feel great joy in dancing, especially to conga drums. I love swimming with wild dolphins off Hawaii's shores. I adore hiking through meadows of wild iris, magenta-colored Indian paint brush, purple fringe, and columbine that only bloom above 10,000 feet in the Colorado Rockies. In winter, I love forging a cross-country ski trail with friends through fresh powder and drinking in the snow-covered peaks in every direction. I could go on, and I'm sure you could make your own list of the things and activities that bring you joy.

But doing the things we love, no matter how much we love them, brings only a fleeting joy. Try as we may to cram every weekend, every vacation, every free moment with the things we love, we still have to return to the rest of our lives: We still have work to do, groceries to buy, bills to pay, and the car to keep running. We still have to wake up four or five times in the night to nurse the infant and get up early to taxi the older kids to school, then get ourselves to work on time. We still have to face conflict in our relationship and money worries. We still have to address the headaches, flu, back pain, illness, and other physical symptoms that life brings our way.

We can't expect to find joy in all this hard stuff. Or can we? I'm here to tell you that we *can*. In fact, if we only expect to find joy while doing what we really love, we end up spending about 90 percent of our lives joyless. And, as you will soon find out, *we* are the ones who limit our joy. That's not only a lousy deal, it's not at all the way it's supposed to be.

In the pages that follow I want to introduce you to a broader, more expanded version of joy. I want to reacquaint you with the unlimited joy that lives deep in your core. Not that over-the-top ecstatic joy we feel after dancing, skiing, or doing what we love all day (though it can be) but the softer, subtler joy that can flood our awareness with a sense of inner peace and well-being, no matter what is happening around us. The ever-present inner joy that allows us to take everything much less seriously.

This book is about how to stop shortchanging ourselves. It's about how to open the door to everyday joy wherever you are, whatever you are doing. Yes, even in the middle of a busy, frustrating, anxiety-ridden day. You see, joy is not something we need to go out and find; joy resides inside us. We arrive with an unlimited supply, deep inside. It's that place in our core that constantly reminds us that, no matter what is happening around us, no matter what is grabbing our attention, we are safe and we are loved.

If this sounds strange or impossible, it's because most of us were trained out of this sense of joy a long time ago. But imagine how your life might change if you knew you could always return to this reservoir of inner joy in all situations, that it's always available to you, and all you have to do is remember it's there. You can do exactly this—in just three simple steps. And it's easier than you think.

As a body-centered therapist, I have witnessed hundreds of clients reconnect with their unstoppable joy. All they had to do was the one thing we avoid like the plague: they had to turn and focus directly on any grief, rage, or fear they had been too scared to face for years. That is, they had to change how they unconsciously allowed the everyday fears, hurts, disappointments, and struggles of life to steal their joy away. As soon as they fully expressed these dark feelings, their inner joy bubbled up from deep inside.

Literally hundreds of men and women, couples and college students, have shared their life stories with me. At first, I bought into the belief that life was *causing them* pain. I thought my job was to help them get a divorce, quit their job, or move to a better climate. But I soon realized that these outer changes brought only a short-lived feeling of joy.

They soon slid back into their old habit of being so consumed by feelings and thoughts that they lost their joy. I saw that, even when we can't control our outer circumstances, we always have a choice about *how we respond*. Instead of habitually avoiding pain and discomfort (our human conditioning), we have the choice to stay present to all our feelings while *responding differently* to them. We have the choice to hold them all in joy.

Over the years, I saw that our own beliefs, fears, and habitual reactions to life limit our joy much more than any spouse, boss, or devastating life experience. I started teaching my clients to carry two questions with them in their daily lives: "Am I feeling joy now? If not, how am I holding my joy away?" I walked into each therapy session and workshop with the goal of helping people reconnect with the essential joy in their core. Over time, my three-step approach evolved:

1. Say yes to what is.
2. Witness your thoughts, feelings, and reactions.
3. Respond differently, with kindness and compassion.

By seeing our old habits clearly and by taking full responsibility for how we respond, we become able to hold all of life's gifts in joy. What do I mean by life's gifts? I mean whatever experience sits on your plate today, whether you like it or not, whether you wanted it or tried to avoid it, whether you deem it pleasant or unbearably uncomfortable. As Buddha taught, it's the ten thousand sorrows *and* ten thousand joys of life that allow us to become mature human beings.

Of course, we don't limit our joy consciously. Nobody pushes away joy on purpose. It's an unconscious habit learned over years of watching our parents and grandparents respond to life through a lens of fear. No matter how much they loved us, our elders weren't able to teach us how to bask in unlimited joy *because they never knew it existed*. For centuries, our ancestors were guided by a set of beliefs that they needed to survive—beliefs about fitting into the mainstream at all costs, hiding their vulnerable feelings, not trusting anyone "different," and fitting themselves into a white patriarchal culture. They were too busy fighting wars and finding ways to feed their families to think about joy.

But times have changed. And whatever beliefs were passed down from our ancestors can be changed. They are, after all, only beliefs, not immutable facts. My own Russian grandfather and Romanian grandmother told their six children they came from Germany. As immigrants to the United States in 1905, they lied to avoid being fired, shamed, or even deported as possible communists. I didn't learn my true ancestry until my early-forties. Finally, all that unexplained shame uncovered in my own therapy process, and my intense fear of "being seen," made sense. My whole being relaxed for the first time.

Many of us learned deep shame at our parents' knee. This was only reinforced by the ministers, priests, and other religious authorities that we looked up to in our youth. From all of them, and from years in school, we learned well *not* to pay attention to our wise inner authority. We learned to care more about how we were perceived than how we felt, and we became frightened to even peek at our messy feelings inside.

I can't even count the number of times I have tenderly invited clients to reconnect with their inner core, only to have them gingerly reply, "I'm afraid to. I'm afraid I'll just find a big empty hole inside. I'm afraid I won't like the miserable nothing I find inside, and I can't handle that." But as I invite them to become curious, and as they move through the anger, sadness, fear, and shame that once felt too overwhelming to face, they are pleasantly surprised to touch joy. Whenever we face the dark feelings we have been avoiding, joy naturally bubbles to the surface.

How I Came to Trust in Our Essential Joy

It took me many years to trust my own joy. I still remember sitting in my parents' dark bedroom in northern Minnesota in the dead of winter. I was barely ten years old. My mother had taken a handful of sleeping pills and kept saying she wanted to die. She blamed my father for not loving her enough. She blamed my teenage brother for not behaving good enough. She blamed our small midwestern town of a thousand people for not being exciting enough. And that night, she blamed me for attending a basketball game with my best friend instead of staying home with her. She was drugged on Valium and sleeping pills, but I had no idea what that meant. All I knew was I needed her alive.

As I sat there terrified that she would die, I wondered to myself what could possibly be so painful and scary about being a grown-up that she would want to leave my family, my life, and me. Of course later I came to understand her depression more fully. I realized with great sorrow that no one ever taught my mother—or the rest of us grown-ups, for that matter—how to find happiness amidst the ups and downs of life. And I committed myself to discovering the path to joy and sharing it with others.

In my early twenties, I plummeted into my own depression. My husband of only two years left to "find himself." Two months later, in

November 1972, I left family, friends, and my hometown to accept my first journalism job in the San Francisco Bay Area, where I knew no one. I felt lost, confused, and lonely. When I tried to look ahead into my future, all I could see was an overwhelming black void. I had never imagined being divorced, especially not by twenty-three.

For a full year, I nursed my depression (and rage) by consuming too much cheap red wine and too many lovers. Terrified of becoming suicidal like my mother, I needed answers, and I needed them fast. Those Sunday sermons by my childhood Lutheran pastor certainly weren't going to cut it—not in the midst of the political unrest and sexual revolution exploding in the San Francisco Bay Area in the early seventies.

I turned to New Age consciousness and Buddhism for answers. I learned about Chinese chi meridians and energy chakras that healed in ways never mentioned by my Western doctor. I went to Buddhism classes taught by a little-known Tibetan who had just fled Chinese domination—Tarthang Tulku Rinpoche. The local tabloid listed classes in such then-unheard-of subjects as tai chi, yoga, aikido, and Feldenkrais work. I dove in. I got my first psychic reading and my first massage. But my heart kept feeling drawn to two arenas: Buddhist teachings and body-centered therapies. During weekly Buddhism classes at the Nyingma Institute in Berkeley, Tarthang Tulku taught me the art of watching my breath and labeling my thoughts, feelings, judgments, and fears, called meditation. Of course, now meditation is as common as blue jeans, but in the early seventies Transcendental Meditation was the main meditation around, practiced by a strange few.

Tarthang Tulku was the first adult to teach me that it was safe to close my eyes and look inside, that I didn't need to be ashamed of what I might find. He taught me to stop letting my mind drag me around by the nose by labeling thoughts and gently returning to my breath. With his funny Tibetan accent, bright red robes, and radiant smile, he taught me to relax with what is. With him as my teacher, I began a serious meditation practice.

Around the same time, I also began Bioenergetics therapy with Eleanor Greenlee in northern California. This form of body-centered therapy, originated by Alexander Lowen, releases blocked chi energy by helping the body fully express stuck feelings. Rather than just talk about feelings, as traditional therapy has us do, Bioenergetics teaches us specific postures that help open up our breathing and release blocked feelings.

At times, Greenlee had me lie on a futon, kick my legs, and say loudly what I was feeling. At first I just laughed, feeling silly and self-conscious. But when I finally did it, I felt this life force flood my whole being. Other times, she had me lean backward over a small, padded stool. Tears flowed as my chest opened. In that office, week after week, kicking and breathing, crying and raging, I found my voice. I felt my own power in ways I had never imagined. My image of myself and what I could accomplish in this lifetime changed, forever. The shy, quiet, deferring female I had been conditioned to be literally shape-shifted into the powerful, creative being that I am (and we all are) inside.

The real shocker, though, was that right after I'd spend a session expressing anger, or grief, or fear, my whole body vibrated, and I would feel this unmistakable sense of ecstasy. At times, after releasing scary feelings I never thought I could face, I'd find myself laughing uncontrollably, grinning until my cheeks hurt. It felt like my whole body was smiling. I'd feel so charged with electricity that I would have to dance for hours at the local club just to unleash all the energy streaming through my body.

The experience affected me so deeply that I soon left my position as editor of a Sunday magazine to pursue my new passion full-time. But the first time the concept of *unlimited joy* really caught my attention was at a Buddhist retreat a few years later. On the fifth day of the retreat, Jack Kornfield gave a dharma talk on "the four unlimited qualities of Buddhism": lovingkindness, compassion, joy, and equanimity. I had certainly known joy—from doing the things I loved—but I became intrigued by the idea that joy could come from just *being*, non-doing. And that it was unlimited. I realized I had experienced *unlimited joy* in my body many times—whenever I fully expressed deep feelings; whenever I presenced myself and basked in the pure joy of Being that is at our core.

Several years later, in 1992, at a training with Gay and Kathlyn Hendricks, I learned how *intentions* hold the power to dissolve our old unconscious beliefs. As I lay on my yoga mat on that conference room floor in Breckenridge, Colorado, I closed my eyes and began taking deep breaths in my belly. Gay was leading the 45-minute breathwork session. He invited all of us to set an intention, to softly tell ourselves what we would like to heal completely. I felt good generally, but I knew I had held chronic tension in my jaw and neck for years. So I whispered to myself, "I am willing to heal my jaw and neck completely." For what felt like an eternity, I kept deep breathing, but nothing happened. I'd had enough powerful experiences not to give up or jump into my head. So I just kept breathing in my belly and completely trusted my body to release whatever it needed to in its own timing.

Suddenly, my jaw began to vibrate. Soon, my whole body shook. Memories of my childhood flushed into my awareness. I recalled hiding under the covers, curled up in a tight ball, afraid to find my depressed mother cold, white, and dead in the morning. I kept deep breathing, knowing my body was releasing waves of stuck fear through the shaking and vibrating. Afterwards, when I sat up, I started giggling uncontrollably. I felt so filled with pure joy that I began skipping around the conference room (this from a forty-year-old professional who hadn't skipped in years!). The tension in my jaw was released. I remained flooded with this joyful exuberance, like a natural high, for several days.

Now I knew in my bones, from my own body experiences, that focusing directly on stuck feelings reconnects us with our joy. But it was by walking my clients through these steps day after day, year after year, that my eyes opened to its far-reaching potential. When Shirley was referred to me by her doctor for uterine cysts, I didn't know if I could help. But I knew I trusted her inner wisdom. I had her lie down and breathe into her belly. I invited her to focus directly on the cysts. She cried within seconds. Soon she spoke about an abortion she had had in her early twenties. Though it was twenty years ago, she still felt plagued by guilt. After surrendering to her grief, and forgiving herself, she reported feeling very awake and alive, more than she had in years. When I saw her some years later, she nonchalantly mentioned that the cysts had disappeared.

David came to see me, complaining of stomach tension "my whole adult life," he said. As he breathed deeply, directly into the center of his belly tension, he touched rage. "I thought I was over that," he said. "But I remember my father criticizing me unrelentingly as a young boy." After releasing his rage, he grieved for the boy who could never do anything good enough in his father's eyes. His stomach tension went away.

Client after client showed me how fully expressing feelings is a gateway to joy. When people find the courage to face whatever they have been avoiding, you can literally *see* aliveness and joy flood their whole being. Their eyes radiate aliveness. Their faces and bodies reveal serenity and inner peace, as if they are now able to handle anything with ease. No longer stuck in the past, no longer afraid to come fully into the present, they expand into the joy-filled Beings that they truly are, as if they had never been hurt or wounded by anyone, ever, in their lives.

To expand into everyday joy, it's important to distinguish between our Inner Self and our Being Self. Our Inner Self (also called ego or personality) is an emotionally young, vulnerable, childlike part of ourselves that reacts with fear to unpredictability, change, and the unknown. It was trained from a young age to seek safety. It takes things too personally and reacts defensively. It needs us to stay consciously connected with it by tuning in and asking what it's feeling and what it needs. It doesn't need us to buy into its fears, which is our habit. It simply needs reassurance from our powerful, creative Being Self, which is our mature, expansive, all-loving, all-compassionate, God-like Essence, the part of us that easily holds all of life in love and joy. Our Being Self is pure consciousness. It has no personal identity, no "I" to protect or defend. It simply is, moment to moment.

Over the years, I have come to trust that my clients, on a Being level, are having exactly the experience they are supposed to be having. When they sit down in my office and voice a complaint, I say, "Good." If someone says, "My back pain is back," I say, "Good. Let's explore why that pain needs your attention. Let's uncover what feeling lives underneath it." Even when a client says, "I'm depressed," if I'm feeling feisty, I say, "Good. Exaggerate that character. Move around the room being depressed. Say its thoughts out loud. Or lie down on this futon, close your eyes, and take some deep breaths. Find that place in your body where you feel depressed. Give it a voice. See what it's trying to teach you." I know that, even though depression is consuming their awareness, it is only a small part of who they are. As they make the depression more conscious, they shift into their Being Self, the one who holds even depression in love.

Why does this work? Because the breath, body, and heart all live in present time. Joy lives in present time. It's the mind (where our awareness is so easily snagged in past memories and future plans) that rarely stays in the present for more than a few seconds. By pausing to take deep breaths, however, we unhook our awareness and bring it into the present. Whenever we *locate a feeling in the body*, we presence ourselves. Whenever we *fully express any feeling*, whether we've sat on it for ten minutes or ten years, we come into the present. Whenever we *acknowledge where we are at in this moment*, we step out of that tight, dark shoebox of past conditioning and return to our inner joy.

Imagine a huge, Universal mother figure holding her arms around your every life experience. That is who you really are. That is your Essence, in the core of your Being. Your center is filled with unlimited love and joy. It's capable of holding whatever life brings you in loving compassion. There is no good or bad, no right or wrong, in your core. No judgment. Like comforting a small child, your Being Self embraces every frustration, every hurt and disappointment, every fear and pain with loving acceptance. As you open the gate, you discover her unlimited capacity.

In the following pages, I will teach you the three simple steps that have been so life changing for my clients and myself—steps you can use anytime you realize you've lost touch with joy. By practicing these steps, you will find that you are finally able to relax into life, amid all the ups and downs of being human. Along the way, these steps show you how to engage your Being Self and the world it will open up for you.

I wrote this book to help you make friends with *all* your feelings— even those that terrify you, and those you never expected to experience in this lifetime. I designed it to accommodate today's fast-paced living. The brief essay format allows you to read a quick "byte" during breakfast or lunch, before bed, or during your commute. After part one, feel free to skip around. Read the essays that best fit where you are right now. Whether you are struggling with hopelessness about the world situation, or frustrated to the breaking point by a whining child, you can apply these three steps and access your core of joy. Whether you feel trapped in your job or desperate about your relationship, use these steps as a map through the wilderness. Whether you are drowning in loneliness or enraged by the driver in front of you, you can come to hold even these experiences in joy. These steps aren't just a new self-help technique; they are a way of living that allows you to be awake to all your feelings, all your experiences, all of life.

I filled the book with examples of how others have opened themselves to inner joy. After an opening set of chapters that explores each of the three steps, you will find a section called "Feeling Habits," where you will learn how to hold feelings such as grief, disappointment, loneliness, fear, shame, anger, and despair in loving compassion. By reading how others have opened their hearts to these painful feelings, and practicing the exercises at the end of each chapter, you will watch your own heart opening to joy. In section three, "Mind Habits," you will see how worry, doubt, judgment, comparing, and obsessive thinking, among other habits, all distance us from experiencing life directly. Though it's impossible to eliminate these age-old patterns, you will learn how to observe them from your mature Being Self, label them, and easily let go of these mind habits that rob you of joy. Section four, "Belief Habits," outlines the core, unconscious belief habits that keep joy away and, in the process, helps you create new, healthy beliefs, ones that are aligned with who you are now. In a final section, called "Jump Starts," you will learn some "quickie" tips for reconnecting with your joy, no matter where you are or what you are doing.

Your only job is to say *yes* to your current experience, to *witness* it and *respond differently*, no matter what anyone around you is doing. Your job is to *keep facing* the layers of hurt, fear, and disappointment that may have built a thick wall around your heart and to *keep choosing joy*, even if the ground under your feet, built on a rickety foundation of old habits, begins to shake.

Of course, dropping familiar defenses can feel very uncomfortable, even threatening, at first. After all, that's why our defenses are created in the first place. Let yourself move slowly into these tender, vulnerable areas. Don't force your deeper feelings. Don't expect too much too fast. And be extra, extra forgiving all those times you slide back into old patterns. Change is never a linear path. In awake moments, you will feel totally able to notice your fears and talk about them to loved ones. Other times, you will hold tightly to old habits, convinced that all this joy talk is just some fluffy Pollyanna gibberish. Hang in there.

Picture yourself crossing a rushing stream from old to new habits. As you move toward the middle, slowly let go of the old, familiar shoreline that appeared to keep you safe up to this point. Move slowly and carefully toward the new shore, knowing that a much more loving and compassionate way of relating to yourself, and to life, is waiting for you on the other side.

And remember, in each moment we essentially have two choices: We can buy into the old fear-based patterns and act them out (again), or we can bravely choose joy. Even in dark moments, gripped by fear, we can whisper to ourselves, "I choose joy—even now." But don't take my word for it. Try it out in your own life. Let your feelings, fears, habits, and beliefs be your new gateway to joy. See what happens.

The Three Steps to Everyday Joy

THERE ARE THREE BASIC INGREDIENTS FOR THIS INNER TRANS-
formation: willingness, curiosity, and courage. *Willingness* allows your
heart, your emotions, your unconscious, and your conscious awareness to align together in the direction of healing. It clears the fog so
you can see yourself clearly. Willingness makes it easier to let go of
unconscious habits. You never need to know *how* you will make the
change (though fear tries to stop you by demanding that you know
how immediately). Willingness engages your body and heart wisdom
and, as you will find out, they are trustworthy guides.

Curiosity, the second ingredient, replaces our habit of judgment
with a kind of childlike wonder. Rather than judging yourself merci-
lessly for having back pain, feeling depressed, or getting sick, you simply
bring a neutral, nonjudgmental attitude to *all* feelings and experiences.
As you wonder, with curiosity, what the depression is about, new ways
of seeing yourself and inner wisdom flood your awareness. As you ask,
"I wonder how I typically react to fear, sadness, or disappointment?"
you see *without judgment* your tendencies to feel anxious, stay busy,
or withdraw when upset. Seeing clearly gives you freedom of choice. As
you shift identities more and more into your Being Self, you allow *all*
feelings to share the same space with love and joy.

Courage is required whenever we step into unknown territory. The
inner terrain of our unconscious is no exception. Courage helps us see
ourselves, and our old habitual reactions, clearly with compassion. Ego
loves to focus only on our successes, blind to the ways our old habits
are hurting ourselves and others. Courage helps us face any pain we've
been avoiding and move forward into the wise, mature Beings that we
are inside.

Step One: Saying Yes to What Is

As a species, we should never underestimate
our low tolerance for discomfort.
—PEMA CHODRON

As I sit down to write this chapter about saying yes to whatever is true in the moment, I realize that my chest feels tight. I'm distracted with thoughts that I could slip into a second round of bronchitis if I'm not careful. I think about how much I hate being sick, and then I'm off and running with thoughts of all I do (and spend) to support my health and how unfair it is that I occasionally get sick anyway. It makes me chuckle. Here I am, writing about saying yes to this moment, and I don't like this moment. My rebellious kid inside smirks at me with her upper lip curled. "Why?" she asks disgustedly. "Why would anyone say yes to being sick? I wanted to ski this morning and create a workshop this afternoon. I have a dinner date. This sucks."

Sound familiar? Nobody wants to be sick, or hurt, or depressed, or feel rejected. And so we resist. We resist whatever we don't like. We resist what frightens us. We resist things that make us uncomfortable. We resist change. We resist the unfamiliar, the unexpected. In fact, as you will see as we look at resistance, we resist most of life.

It's human nature. We love feeling "good," but we resist "negative" feelings like the plague. We love the honeymoon stage of relationship, but as soon as we smell conflict brewing in our relationship, we start thinking that we might be with the wrong person. In short, we love getting what we want, and go to great lengths to avoid discomfort.

Unfortunately, by resisting "negative" feelings, we paradoxically shut down our capacity for joy. Buddha explained this human dilemma over 2,500 years ago. He told his students about our propensity for clinging to pleasure and avoiding discomfort. He taught that this aspect of human conditioning is how we create more suffering for ourselves.

I'm sure, though, that Buddha had no idea of the lengths we would go to in order to avoid pain and discomfort: Antidepressants. Anti-anxiety pills. Over-the-counter painkillers. Over-the-counter soda pop, injected with caffeine. Espresso stands at every street corner, mini-mall, and airport. Legal and illegal drugs. High-speed, off-road vehicles. Satellite TV. Twenty-four-hour access to the Internet and porn. The list goes on and on.

After all, who has time to bother feeling sad or lonely if we can get rid of it with a pill? Who wants to feel any "negative" feeling if we can push a button and lose ourselves in mindless entertainment? Who wants to bother becoming a more compassionate, loving spouse if we can just file our own divorce papers and jump into bed with someone new? Who wants to heal our poor, aching planet if we can keep stockpiling more personal wealth? Who wants to "wake up" to the soft, vulnerable beings we are inside when we have so many ways to distract ourselves? Resistance looks easier, and a whole lot more fun. But it carries a whopping price tag.

Resistance is so insidious and pervasive that we don't even know when we are resisting. Most of the time, we sleepwalk through our life, planning the next exciting moment instead of feeling this present one fully. When we don't like the present, our knee-jerk habit is to distance ourselves from it by judging it as good or bad.

"No. Not *that*. Not *me*. Not *now*. This can't be happening to me. I'm not ready yet. I hate being sick. I can't be depressed—that only happens to other people. If only *he* hadn't cheated on me, if only I could look the other way . . . Let me savor the hot sex a little longer before I have to deal with conflict in my relationship. Let me finish writing my book before the cancer disables me." This is how resistance sounds inside our heads.

Life Expands and Contracts Along with the Universe

To stop creating suffering for ourselves, we need to better understand how things work. The Universe moves in continuous waves of expansion and contraction. Ocean waves expand and contract. The phases of the moon expand and contract. Our breath and heartbeat expand and contract. Our bank accounts expand and contract. Our health and creative expression expand and contract. We feel blessed, on top of the world during the times of expansion. Yet, when our lives contract, we act surprised, even indignant. We think that the Universe is playing some mean trick on us, picking on us.

When the economy contracts, and recession follows, we contract in fear. We want to blame someone, as if we're not supposed to feel down sometimes, or ever. Behind closed doors, we exclaim, "It's just not fair!" But in truth, we are simply experiencing the natural ebb and flow of the Universe.

David sat in my office stubbornly exclaiming, "I want a divorce." It was his and his wife's second couple's session. "I tried to tell you for a whole year what wasn't working for me," he said, glaring at his wife, "and you wouldn't listen. You never listen. You always interrupt me. You always override what I want with your wants. I'm tired of it."

Of course, the "D" word gets everyone's attention. Sara quickly apologized for her habit of overriding him. She begged him for one more chance. He agreed. In individual therapy, she came face to face with her fear of abandonment—the fear that had successfully sabotaged her two previous marriages. She finally saw all the ways that she had been unconsciously pushing David away. Suddenly, she identified the culprit causing this havoc. "I hate hearing no. Ever since I was a kid, I've been terrified of feeling rejected. But look, Carolyn," she smiled, "now I have to deal with the big N-O as in David doesn't want me anymore." She broke down and cried. "I've spent my entire life jumping through hoops, trying to control people, anything to avoid hearing no."

After facing that fear and being willing to see it when it arose, her desperate need to control David dissolved. She was able to listen to his needs and feelings and respond with love. He felt the shift immediately. Now comes the interesting part. Sara's shift brought David's own mistrust into the spotlight. An abused boy, David felt suspicious of anyone who said, "I love you." He had trouble trusting her change. "She's just doing this because I threatened divorce," he confided. During an individual session, he realized how terrified he was of letting love in. As he breathed directly into this gripping fear in his heart, it released. He stopped holding Sara at arm's length. He stopped needing to find fault with her to hold her love away. In their last couple's session, he said, "I can't divorce her now! Things are going better than they ever have between us."

We all have our favorite ways of buying into fear and holding love away. Whatever is true in the moment, we often want it somehow to be different, better, easier, more in our favor. After each hurt or disappointment, fear convinces us to resist life even more. Staying safe takes precedence over everything else, including our own joy and aliveness. Resistance becomes a way of protecting our hearts in an unpredictable, changing world.

Unfortunately, we pay a high price for fast forwarding through the uncomfortable parts. Whenever we judge feelings as "negative" or "bad" to avoid discomfort, we cheat ourselves out of receiving life's gifts. As the saying goes, "What we resist, persists." Worse yet, we lose aliveness and rob ourselves of joy. We grow more and more loyal to the voice of fear, which always sounds so practical and reasonable. But it's still just fear.

Surrendering Our False Sense of Control

These days our world is changing so rapidly, it's hard to keep up. Amid such rapid changes, familiarity can offer some sense of control, even if it's a false sense. We human beings cling to what we know, even if "familiar" is hurting us, or stopping us from growing up. In this fast-paced life, it's easier to pretend, to ourselves and others, that we're not really vulnerable, tender human beings. We like to believe that, if we're just clever enough, if we just play the game right, if we're smarter than the next person, if we exercise and eat right, if we have enough money, we can avoid pain and discomfort.

But experiencing suffering doesn't mean that something is wrong. The Buddha taught that one way to stop creating more suffering for ourselves is to stop resisting what is. He wasn't just speaking to some of us. He was speaking to *all* of us. The truth is, we can use every experience (good or bad) to wake up.

Unfortunately, most of us were never told this. No one said that living our lives completely means letting all of life flow through us—the joy and sorrow, the pain and discomfort. Instead, we learned to identify with our young, defended, less mature egos. We learned to listen to the stories our egos tell us. We bought into the human conditioning that's been passed down for centuries: that pleasure is good and pain is bad. We've gotten used to our egos convincing us that, by resisting and denying our pain, we are better than all those people out there struggling. This blinded thinking cuts us off from our heart's deeper wisdom. It blocks us from connecting with our pure joy of Being.

Resistance Comes with a Hefty Price Tag

If I didn't know better, I'd say, "Go for it! Avoid all the pain you can for as long as you can." If I hadn't witnessed the elaborate suffering we cause ourselves by resisting discomfort, I'd keep quiet. But I've seen too much. Clients and students have shown me time and again the physical illness and emotional pain we cause ourselves by resisting what is. There is Paula, whose migraines went away when she stopped hiding behind confusion and began writing her novel. There is Linda, who rediscovered her joy when she faced her guilt and grief about having an abortion. There is Neal, who uncovered joy for the first time when he expressed his rage and fear about being molested.

Jack Kornfield tells us in *A Path with Heart*, "When we come into the present . . . we encounter whatever we have been avoiding. We must have the courage to face whatever is present—our pain, our desires, our grief, our loss, our secret hopes, our love—everything that moves us most deeply." Whether we agonize over a stubbed toe or are immersed in dark depression, a mild cold, or money fears, the healthy direction is facing whatever is true directly. It's never as scary as it looks peering out from the starting line.

Dissolving Resistance

This is all about saying yes to what is. Saying yes dissolves resistance instantly. It empowers us. Saying yes helps us stand on both feet and find the courage to handle whatever arrives on our plate today. It blows the town whistle, alerting our inner wisdom to rush to our aid.

Saying yes teaches us that we are safe to be totally honest—with ourselves and our loved ones: "Yes, I am feeling depressed and sad today, and yes, it is scary to feel this way." When we say yes to what is, love and acceptance share the same space with whatever we are feeling. It says, "I love myself for feeling depressed and sad, and for hating feeling depressed." Yes reassures our tender, vulnerable Inner Self that "I can handle it, even this." It engages our curiosity to wonder, "What is my body, and my heart, trying to tell me here?" When we say yes, we don't need to come up with white lies to defend, protect, or align with our ego.

Slowly, as we keep saying yes to what is, our vulnerable Inner Self begins to trust life. We start to trust that we are having exactly the experience we are supposed to be having. It may not be the one we expected. It may trigger varying degrees of fear and discomfort at times. But we say yes anyway. Soon, each issue on our plate feels more workable, more manageable.

For example, Jed and Sara came to see me for couple's counseling eight years ago. She wanted to break up. He acquiesced. But Jed was terrified to grieve this huge loss. Instead, he drank more. He dated several different women with no intention to commit to anyone. His ego convinced him, "I didn't need her. I don't need anybody." This plan worked for two years. But Jed came back to therapy. His need to grieve had grown so intense, he was having panic attacks. Alcohol wasn't working. Even the casual sex became boring after a while. He needed to face his pain.

In my office, as he closed his eyes and breathed deeply, he felt a tightness around his heart. He quietly wiped the tears from his cheeks. "I haven't cried in forty years," he admitted. I encouraged him to keep breathing directly down into the tightness in his chest. Tears kept flowing. When he was done, his eyes met mine. His eyes looked radiant, as if he had released a lifetime of sorrow. "I feel good," he said with a huge grin. "I feel all bubbly and happy inside. I'll have to cry more often." As he stood up to leave, he added, "You know that fear that came up so strong at the beginning of our session—the fear that nobody will ever love me. It's gone. So is the heavy pressure in my chest."

This habit of resisting "negative" feelings is so deeply ingrained in us, it often just feels like that is how life *is*. It takes steady work and focused attention to shift it. I know I still work at it, whispering yes under my breath whenever I think of it. Whenever I notice my mind running wild with some fear of the future or difficult memory from the past, I say yes to it and feel it dissolve.

Resisting Feelings Forces Us to Act Them Out

Nobody walks around saying, "I'm going to resist life now." We don't start the day declaring, "I think I'll rob myself of joy today." That's the problem. We don't think about it at all. It's an "unconscious" habit. It occurs below our awareness. We learned to bypass "negative" feelings, and we just keep doing it. We think we can avoid conflict in our relationships by withholding feelings that might trigger anger. We believe we are protecting ourselves from future disappointment and hurt by making "practical, reasonable" choices. But all we are really doing is acting out our feelings unconsciously.

When we say yes to what is, we see clearly, with loving eyes, our own personalized version of resistance. We are creatures of habit, even if that habit is robbing our joy. Lori desperately wanted to get married and have a baby. By thirty-eight, her biological clock was screaming. When Bill appeared, she fell madly in love. But six months later, when he proposed, she froze. She pulled her "judgment" card out—the same card she had used to get rid of five earlier candidates. She judged him for being "too unconscious, too insensitive, too unskilled at sharing his feelings." In angry moments, she flat-out told him he would make a lousy father. She was buying into her judgment and acting it out. In therapy, I invited her to notice her judgment, label it "judging, judging," and let it go. She resisted. She didn't believe she was judging him. But she agreed to try it for two weeks.

She came back to therapy two weeks later a changed woman. "Wow!" she grinned, wide-eyed. "I did it. I labeled my judgments. And it felt like I saw Bill, and myself, for the first time. I ended up telling him how terrified *I* am about picking the wrong man and being stuck with a tiny baby. I also owned how scared *I* am about not being a good mother. Most of all, though," she added, "I'm afraid of getting the love I've always wanted." The two married last August. And they adore their two-month-old baby.

We are all in human bodies sharing similar experiences and feelings. Daily, life experiences move through us that trigger feelings totally out of our control. Most of the time, we are unaware what we are feeling inside. One experience triggers calmness. The next triggers intense anxiety. A newspaper article might trigger money worries, or despair. Our spouse's ailing health might trigger fear and helplessness. All these are out of our control. What is in our control is how we respond. If we break through resistance by saying yes to what is, we give ourselves the freedom of choice. Loving ourselves for whatever we are feeling puts the brakes on our unconscious habit of resisting life.

Taking Self-Responsibility

An important shift occurs when you say yes to life. Besides breaking the pattern of resistance, you discover the tremendous freedom to be found in taking responsibility. Rather than believing "life outside me" is causing my frustration, pain, or loneliness, you begin seeing the huge role your own reaction to life plays in your happiness.

The simple act of saying yes to what is helps us make friends with ourselves, and life. It's one of the best gifts we can give ourselves. As our own self-awareness deepens, we come to see that what our mind expects, and what our actual experience is, rarely coincide. The mind measures life against an "ideal" perspective, which means that most of life, including who we are and what we have accomplished, is not good enough. What a cruel habit.

When we say yes to what is, it feels like waking up from a long sleep. We stop responding with the same beliefs, attitudes, and judgments that we inherited as children, when our heartfelt wisdom was much less developed. We stop sleepwalking through our relationships and recognize that each day, each moment, is too precious to withdraw and withhold feelings for four years (or four days, or four minutes, for that matter).

Suddenly our eyes see more clearly—as if some invisible blindfold has been removed. Our ears have more space to hear the music of daily life, including the voices of those we love. Suddenly, all those plans, thoughts, doubts, and judgments whirling through our minds carry much less weight. There's much more breathing room—in our day, in our relationship, in our feelings and longings. We slow down. We take deeper breaths. We stop to *really* notice that blue spruce towering outside the patio window.

And we know, in our hearts, that we are good enough, just as we are. Even in this moment—if our bodies are experiencing illness or our hearts struggle with loneliness—we can remind ourselves that, deep in our hearts, we are safe and we are loved, no matter what. When we dare to touch this tender soft spot in our core, we remember that being lovable is not something we have to strive for or earn. It's who we are. The more we respond to life from this loving place, the more we can soften and trust the process of life. And the more we can lean into life's mysteries, even the painful parts, with joy.

Practice with the following tools until they become your familiar way of responding to life. Take your time; it's not a race. It took you years to build up your resistance. Give yourself at least the next few weeks to become familiar with the ways you resist life—in your body— and to begin to say yes to it all.

Practice Tools:

1. The easiest place to identify resistance is in our bodies. Most of us resist such common symptoms as a headache, neck and shoulder tension, back pain, and stomach tension. As an experiment, take five minutes to lie on your back with a pillow under your knees, close your eyes, and deep breathe in your belly. After several deep breaths, let your awareness move slowly down your body, scanning it. Notice and *hear* whatever is true in your body in this moment. Also, notice any resistance to or judgment of the tightness, tension, numbness, or pain that you don't want to be feeling. Say yes to whatever you are noticing. Often, focusing our attention on tension and pain decreases its intensity.

2. Now take a few moments to deep breathe in your belly and notice any feelings inside. Say yes to whatever feelings might be up for you

without judging them. Just notice. If you feel sadness or tiredness, acknowledge it to yourself. Promise yourself a time, later, to be with those feelings. Saying yes to whatever you are feeling throughout the day allows the feeling to simply flow through you.

3. Setting an intention is a powerful tool to counteract habits, which I first learned from Gay and Kathlyn Hendricks. Before getting out of bed, place one hand over your heart and one hand over your belly. Say, "I'm willing to say yes to whatever feelings come up for me today." Or, "I'm willing to say yes to any tension in my body today and hear what that symptom is trying to tell me." Also make a commitment to yourself to share your feelings with your partner, friend, or loved one.

Step Two: Witnessing Ourselves

*Those who have not found their true wealth,
which is the radiant joy of Being and the deep,
unshakable peace that comes with it, are
beggars, even if they have great wealth.*
—ECKHART TOLLE

When it comes to feelings, our bodies have to act them out unconsciously, even if our egos are busy denying them. What few of us realize is that our bodies are incapable of lying. If we feel sad but fail to say, "I feel sad," our bodies will find a way to act out our sadness by pouting, sulking, or withdrawing. They have to. If we feel jealous but fail to say, "I notice my jealousy got triggered while you were talking to your ex," our bodies are forced to act out our jealousy. We can lie about our feelings, even to ourselves. But our bodies cannot. They have to act out our true feelings.

We can be highly creative, or downright boring, in acting out our feelings—we sulk, we pout, we slam doors, we yell, we stay silent or stay busy, we work late, we withhold sex. Some of us even have a secret affair, or think about it. But all this acting out takes hours, days, months, even years. On the other hand, saying, "I feel hurt" takes two seconds. Our young ego self doesn't like to admit "vulnerable" feelings such as hurt or fear. It resorts to defensive anger or self-righteous indignation, and it's happy to take years to act this out, if it has to. Our Being Self, on the other hand, holds no judgments about any feelings. It's happy to say, "I feel sad or hurt" and step back into its true nature as quickly as possible: open, compassionate love and joy.

That's where *witnessing* comes in. Witnessing is the new kid on the block. It's so new, most of us have never heard of it. That's why it takes effort to witness our feelings and reactions. It takes awareness. We can act out or deny our feelings in our sleep, these are so ingrained in our unconscious. But it takes courage, and willingness, to see our old habits clearly (the last thing ego wants to admit). Just as many of us learned to make "I" statements years ago to save our relationships, witnessing is the next step.

Witnessing Shifts Our Perspective

Witnessing is shifting our perspective. It's expanding our awareness of what it means to be a human being in a body. It's relating differently to the less mature part of us who blames, defends, judges, doubts, compares, has to be right, takes things too personally, and acts out. Witnessing is happily trading in this young "I" self for our mature, powerful, expanded Being Self—once we know how to get there. It's seeing the engaging movie called *My Life* through a wide-angle lens after spending most waking moments placing our every word, thought, and action under a microscope. It's honoring the pure joy that compassion brings, as Tarthang Tulku teaches, by bringing it to ourselves, first.

Witnessing is stepping beyond the accepted definition of "grown-up" into a new, inner frontier. It's taking ourselves less seriously. It's being less "caught up" by whatever issue sits on our plate today, and whatever feelings those issues trigger. It's welcoming fear and hope, happiness and sorrow, all equally. Simultaneously, it's remembering that who we are, in our core, is so much bigger, more gracious and loving than whatever thoughts or feelings are moving through us. It's stopping ourselves mid-thought, mid-sentence to feel and *talk about* our fear or sadness rather than acting them out.

It's relaxing into what is, no matter what it is, with awareness and compassion.

For example, let me witness myself in this moment. I am writing at my desk with an ice pack on my left knee. I "notice" the me who hates being injured or limited in any way. Rather than unconsciously acting out my hatred of limitation by pouting all day, I remember to say yes to my left knee being injured and yes to hating limitation. As I close my eyes and tune inside, I notice some resentment that my injured knee prevented me from mountain biking last weekend. I don't let the resentment dominate my mood. Instead, I take two seconds to acknowledge it. By acknowledging *all* feelings that are present, I relax into my Being Self, which holds all my feelings in compassionate joy.

It's a freer, healthier, friendlier way to travel through life. It allows much more space for joy. Forgiveness and compassion put breathing room around whatever we are experiencing. At times it's like a breath of fresh air. Other times, it feels challenging.

However, witnessing can only occur *after* we look directly at our old habits and reactions.

The best way I know to teach you about witnessing is to give you a body experience of it. The next time you feel angry, take a few moments to close your eyes and breathe deeply into your belly. Even allow the anger to feel more intense. Take one imaginary step backward inside your skin and *watch* the part of you that is consumed by anger. Be curious. Notice how anger feels in your body. Notice how your mind justifies feeling angry, makes itself feel right. Step out of your habit of being totally caught up in the anger and open to this fresh look. Drop any judgments about whether anger is good or bad. Let the anger be there without needing to get rid of it or fix it in any way.

Now see whether anger broadens or narrows your vision. Peek underneath the anger and notice whether sadness, hurt, disappointment, or fear are fueling it. Try this same experiment with frustration, loneliness, despair, and resentment—all your feelings.

In the process, you cultivate awareness of two parts of yourself simultaneously—the young ego self who is consumed by the anger and has to be right, and your Being Self, who is watching anger move through you *with compassion.* Imagine holding this angry reaction in unconditional love, the way a mother holds her crying infant, confident that the baby will stop crying as its needs are met and it feels loved. The very second we watch our young ego self feel angry, scared, sad, or lonely, we no longer believe that is who we are in that moment. We have expanded awareness into our Being Self. This broad net of unlimited love and joy catches us every time we let go of the "story" in our minds.

However, this shift in awareness can trigger anxiety at first. Our young ego selves immediately demand to know, "But, but, but . . . if I'm not my clever thoughts, and if I'm not my intense feelings, then who am I? If I'm not this great personality I spent years building up, who am I?" What a great question! The truth is, we are not our feelings—though feelings certainly move through us. We are not our thoughts—though thoughts vie for our attention constantly. We are not even our beliefs—though we held tight for years to those beliefs (ones that promised to keep us safe as children).

Our gentle, compassionate Being loves to answer the question, "Who Am I?," especially when we are feeling expanded, and willing to listen. In certain respects, our Being waits patiently our whole lives to share its deep inner wisdom with us. "Who you are, in your core, is so much bigger than whatever you are feeling or thinking in any given moment, or whoever you were taught you were," our Being whispers gently. "You are unlimited love, joy, kindness, and compassion." Witnessing reconnects us with our essential Being Self.

A delightful mother of four bounced into my office last week, grinning nonstop after "witnessing" herself for the past seven days. "Why am I so happy?" Connie asked. "And why was it so easy to make healthy choices this week? Because I didn't drink any alcohol, and I didn't want to drink any alcohol. I put *my* needs first instead of running around answering to my husband's every little request. My whole life, I felt unwanted. I stayed too long in two unhealthy marriages just because I felt nobody else wanted me."

"You tell me," I encouraged. "What shifted inside as you practiced witnessing?" She closed her eyes to think. "I didn't buy into all that self-loathing I've been afraid to face for years. When it came up, I *witnessed* those painful, unwanted feelings, as if they were a small part of me. I tuned into what the feeling felt like in my body. Then I held my pain with the same love that I hold my little four-year-old in when he's upset."

In other words, her perspective shifted. Instead of acting out her unwanted feelings (as she had done for forty-some years), she witnessed them from her Being Self. From this place, it felt natural to give her unwanted feelings what they had always longed for and never received from her parents or husband—loving, compassionate acceptance.

Putting Space around Our Feelings and Thoughts

Witnessing puts space around whatever we are feeling and thinking at any given moment. It is holding our pain and sorrow, resentment and fear in the nurturing embrace of unconditional love—the love we are all capable of in our core. The second we witness our experience, we remind ourselves that, under all circumstances, we are joyful Beings who happen to be feeling _____ as we move through the Universe.

Witnessing is a gift to ourselves. It gifts us with awareness. And awareness gives us the freedom to make healthy choices. Sometimes just taking one minute to close our eyes and acknowledge, inside, how tired we are makes us feel less tired. It wakes us up out of the old habit of always pushing ourselves to do more. Or we *choose* to take a ten-minute power nap to refresh ourselves. If we have to keep pushing, to meet a deadline, we may promise ourselves a hot bath later. All three are *conscious* choices, made from listening to what is true in our bodies in this moment. All three return us to inner joy.

Through witnessing our human experiences moment to moment (those we like and those we don't like), we come to know ourselves more intimately. We give ourselves, and our lives, much more breathing room. We shift identities from the small me, consumed by fear or lost in thought, to the huge me holding everything in loving acceptance. We put space around whatever we are feeling, thinking, and experiencing. Or we forget to put space around our feelings and thoughts, fall back into acting them out one more time, and hold even our forgetting in kindness and compassion. Gradually, we see our waking life as a dream—a dream nudging us toward reconnecting with Essence.

Talking about Feelings Saves Hours, Days, Even Years

Witnessing forces us to be aware of what we are feeling. It feels like standing on the sidelines, watching our young ego self be consumed by anger, sadness, or fear. It also lets us become aware of the thoughts that are triggered by these feelings. Then we can describe our feelings as the *watcher* rather than the one caught up in feelings.

Let's view an example. We know what it's like to be lost in anger. In our better moments, when we're not throwing dishes across the room, we might blurt out, "I'm so angry, I could scream! If something doesn't change soon here, I'm leaving!"

The same communication, couched in a witnessing framework, might be, "When you said that, *I noticed* fierce anger rise up from my belly. It's burning in my throat. *I notice thoughts* about leaving, about not being able to tolerate this relationship anymore. *What I need in this moment is* _____ (to be held and listened to, to hear some reassuring words, to be told that you love me, or to walk around the block and cool off).

Any time an issue triggers feelings in us (which are usually deeper feelings from a past wound), it's an opportunity to know ourselves more intimately. If we have the courage to share our inner experience in this new way, by witnessing it, we are dropping below the content of the conflict to heal whatever is asking to be healed. We also teach loved ones about our interior world in a nondefensive way that allows deeper closeness.

By noticing and *talking about* our feelings, we connect with our Being Self and speak from there. The communication is much more loving and less defensive than our old ways of acting out, which makes it far easier to receive. For instance, imagine that your mate just blurted out that he or she desperately needs a weekend alone, and you react with fear.

- Close your eyes, tune inside and notice where you feel the fear in your body (it may be a tightness in your diaphragm or butterflies in your belly).

- In a neutral tone, *describe* where you feel the fear in your body and what sensations you notice, as if you are just sharing information: "I'm feeling some fear about being alone this weekend. I notice it as a tightness in my belly, like a tight fist." (You simply share what you see and feel inside, without needing to make your mate's need bad or your fear wrong.) By describing the feeling *without any judgment*, you let it be held in loving acceptance.
- Now, focus directly on the fear and ask this part of you what it needs. (Asking open questions like this, and letting go of thoughts, accesses your inner wisdom.)
- Then say your needs out loud: "I need you to hold me right now and tell me that I'll be OK." Keep stating your needs until they feel met.

Through challenging times in a relationship, most of us have thoughts such as, "This isn't working for me" or, "I need to leave." It's common. We rarely share them, though, for fear of upsetting the other person. *Talking about* our tender, vulnerable feelings creates a safe, sacred setting to describe even these fears in a healthy, nonthreatening way. Instead of acting out by threatening an affair, saying, "I notice I'm having thoughts about having an affair, which signals me that I need to share my feelings with you."

It's critical to be patient with yourself, and your partner, as you flop back and forth between acting out old habits and remembering to talk about your inner truth. For example, Paul and Joann engaged my help as their relationship transitioned from acting out feelings to witnessing them. As a survivor of molestation, Joann had difficulty trusting anybody with her feelings. Instead she resorted to explosive anger. Paul, on the other hand, felt baffled by all feelings and froze whenever Joann yelled or cried.

"Are you willing to try an experiment?" I inquired.

"Yes!" Joann jumped in.

"Since you are at a painful stalemate, I want to ask each of you to exaggerate your position," I continued. "Joann, you get this left half of the room to indulge your despair and anger and hopelessness. Paul, you get the right half of my office to freeze like a deer in the headlights and exaggerate your fear of rejection. Don't think too hard. Just say the thoughts of your character out loud and express its posture, as if you were in a play."

Joann slumped down in her chair, holding her head in her hands, shaking her head. "It's useless," she said. "He never listens to me. He always wants to fix me, like one of his machines, so he can get outside for a run. Nobody ever cares about my feelings."

Paul, meanwhile, is turning the doorknob to head out the door. "Fine," he mumbles. "If she doesn't want my help, I don't need this."

Before he disappeared, I called out, "*Freeze* right where you are. Close your eyes, take some deep breaths, and notice what feeling is fueling this familiar behavior."

"It's hopelessness," Joann said, crying. "I feel an intense pressure in my upper chest. I hate this feeling. I've gone to great lengths to avoid it all my life because it reminds me of when my uncle was molesting me and nobody believed me."

Later, Paul shared his feelings. "I feel like a failure," he said. "My first wife kept telling me what a failure I was until I believed her. Now, when I can't fix Joann's pain, I feel worthless." Joann reached out to comfort him. They held each other.

"Good work," I interjected. "You just did the hardest part—identifying the feeling fueling your old behavior, locating it in your body, and describing it to each other. The last step is to look into each other's eyes and tell each other what you need around this."

Joann spoke. "It's hard for me to know what I need, let alone risk exposing it," she said. "But just now, when I asked my heart what I need, it said to have you hold me and reassure me that you're not leaving. That, and listen to my feelings."

Paul nodded in agreement. "And if you can say *one thing* I'm doing right," he added, "my feelings of worthlessness disappear."

Over the next several weeks, Paul and Joann practiced witnessing. They both expressed frustration at how hard it is, in the middle of intense feelings, to remember to talk about their experience. Joann said how risky it felt inside to tell Paul her needs. I encouraged her to say her "whole" truth: "Create a sacred container for yourself by telling him that you have something to share *and* how scary it is to tell him."

Paul tended to beat himself up inside when he fell back into his pattern, but eventually he became so skilled at witnessing that, right in the middle of acting rejected one night, he paused and told Joann, "Don't believe a word I'm saying—it's Rejected Paul talking." They both burst out laughing, and the conflict ended on the spot.

Unconscious Habits Come Early in Life and Stay Too Long

All of us know how to *un*consciously react to life. "Unconscious" refers to the thoughts, feelings, beliefs, and behaviors that occur below our conscious awareness. As infants, we smiled when we were getting fed and cried when we were hungry, wet, cold, or tired. Life was simple. But as children we gravitate toward what appears to bring safety and love, even if it means disconnecting from our Being Self.

As young children, we learned to explode in anger to get our way, as Dad did, or to withdraw into silence, deciding that anger is bad. Some of us found that crying helped us get our needs met; others quit crying to avoid getting yelled at, or hit. Sometimes feelings felt safe to share with one or both parents, or we kept them to ourselves and learned to judge ourselves for having those feelings at all. We learned to trust others with our soft, vulnerable selves, or we learned that nobody can be trusted. No matter what our situation, we made "rules about life" to cope with the overwhelming and confusing experience of living in a grown-ups' world. These rules were made by a child's undeveloped mind.

Unfortunately, after we mature into adulthood, our young ego self carries these rules about life inside, below our awareness. We wind up unconsciously applying them to current situations without even realizing it. These rules keep reappearing in new variations until we are willing to see ourselves, and our old survival habits, more clearly.

The toughest challenge about witnessing is facing these old rules, and the unconscious feelings fueling them, that we've gone along with for years. It was too painful to face these uncomfortable feelings in the first place, which is why we started avoiding them, and we've been running away from them ever since. The key is to turn and face our fears, and hold all these feelings in compassion.

Most of us judge ourselves, and our humanness, harshly. We buy into the self-doubt, shame, and fear instilled in us in childhood as if they were the real Ten Commandments. And we do this without knowing it. It happens unconsciously. If I hadn't sat in my office the past twenty years hearing people's pain, I never would have believed this. But as I taught people to hold their judgment, doubt, fear, and shame in loving acceptance, I saw first-hand how cruelly we treat ourselves without realizing it.

Witnessing allows our unconscious habits to surface in broad daylight. Seeing these clearly, with kindness and compassion, brings freedom. The "stories" of who did what when to us don't matter much in the end. What does matter is that we reconnect with our Being Self, and hold all aspects of our humanness in a mother's loving embrace. As we bring kindness and compassion to our own humanness, we can put more breathing room around others' imperfections, and hold them, too, in kindness and compassion.

Witnessing is being present. As Buddhism says, we allow the ten thousand sorrows and ten thousand joys of life to flow through, accepting the paradox of life. It's noticing the baby iris buds opening in spring—and noticing the pain of loneliness from deep inside. It's taking two minutes to really look into our Beloved's eyes when we connect. It's cuddling in the morning before our minds pull us out of bed to do something "important."

When we practice the art of witnessing, we lose the need to avoid discomfort. We pause. We wait. We breathe. We remember to take a few long, deep breaths in our belly, signaling our bodies that everything is OK just the way it is. We notice, with curiosity, *whatever* is in our space each moment. We check inside several times a day and notice, without judgment, what feelings are moving through our bodies now. We talk about our feelings with loved ones, trusting that such sharing creates deeper intimacy and closeness. We value closeness—with ourselves and with others.

Witnessing is the ongoing practice of remembering Who We Are, in our core. It's stepping back gently to hold our anger, fear, sadness, and resentment in love and joy. And when we forget, which we will from time to time, it's holding our forgetting and all our human imperfections in the unconditional love of a mother's embrace. It's getting lost in old habits, projecting our fears onto others—but then telling the other person, as soon as we recognize it, that that's what we did. Instead of ditching all our "bad" feelings, it's holding the full gamut of human experience in joy and unconditional love.

As we practice witnessing, our identity shifts. Our defended young ego self retreats, allowing our Being Self to fill our awareness. Whether ecstatic happiness or deep sorrow is moving through us in this moment, our compassionate Being loves all equally. No judgment. No preferences. No right or wrong. No good or bad. All experiences are greeted and held in the unconditional love that is our core nature. That's the heart of everyday joy.

Practice Tools:

1. Practice witnessing your thoughts. Set aside ten or fifteen minutes each day to quiet yourself, close your eyes, take five to ten deep breaths, and gently notice which thoughts are running through your head. (Unless you meditate regularly, you may feel overwhelmed at

first with the zillions of thoughts racing through your mind! Just hang in there.) Your mind may be planning a summer outing, reminiscing about last night's romantic dinner, or obsessing about work. Whatever thoughts are present, stop buying into them. In fact, don't even let your mind finish its sentence. Just label it, "thinking, thinking" and bring yourself back to the in and out of your breath.

2. After you have practiced witnessing your thoughts for a few weeks, try witnessing your feelings. Several times throughout the day, close your eyes, drop your awareness into your body, and notice without judgment what feelings are present. Rather than buying into anger, fear, resentment, or sadness and feeling consumed by it, witness it. If you feel tired, acknowledge, "I feel tired." Take a few seconds to *really feel* how tired you are. If you notice sadness or fear, acknowledge that. If you feel calm and peaceful, acknowledge that. In other words, acknowledge whatever feelings you are noticing. Witnessing feelings frees your body from having to act them out.

3. Now, to deepen the witnessing process, imagine taking one step back from yourself inside so that you are watching the part of you that feels sad—as if two people live inside you: the young Inner Self who is sad, and the Being Self who is holding the sadness in unconditional love. (This takes getting used to without feeling schizoid!) Try helping the *watcher* whisper kind, reassuring words to your Inner Self, such as, "I hear how sad you feel. When things quiet down, I promise to tune in to your feelings." For five minutes, surrender fully to the sadness. Really feel how sad you are. Make a sound that matches how sad you feel. As you grow more comfortable with the process, try showing compassion to scarier feelings, such as rage, shame, resentment, hopelessness, and despair.

4. Set an intention. Setting an intention is a quick, powerful way to change old unconscious habits. It engages our whole being in the direction we want to move. And it's simple. An intention sounds like, "I'm willing to *notice and talk about* my feelings today rather than act them out." It might be very specific, such as, "I'm willing to see clearly what triggers my anxiety," or very general, such as, "I'm willing to make healthy choices." Pick an issue in your current life, or a new behavior you want to adopt, and repeat the intention five to ten times under your breath. After you repeat the intention, begin stating it as if it's already true. Change "I'm willing to . . ." to "I easily notice and talk about my feelings," or "I see clearly what triggers my anxiety." (Even though your mind balks because it's not true *yet*,

this message is received by your heart and the energetic shift begins to take place immediately.) The best time to set an intention is when you first wake up in the morning. Lie on your back and repeat your intention several times. If you wake up too late to do it in the morning, take a few minutes in the middle of the day to close your eyes and whisper the intention several times.

5. *Talk about* your feelings. Talking about your feelings can feel like learning a new language at first. It requires patience. But after you breeze through a few disagreements *not* acting out your feelings, it spurs you on to practice more. First, set an intention each morning. When you first wake up, repeat to yourself, "I'm willing to talk about my feelings today." Then, whenever you notice a feeling inside, see it as an opportunity to practice talking about your feelings. Instead of acting out your fear unconsciously, try saying, "I notice when you said you wanted to travel to Ireland alone, my fear of abandonment got triggered. I experience it as a tightness in my chest. I notice thoughts such as 'nobody cares about my needs ...' What I need is ____ (to hear reassuring words)." Talking about our feelings is taking full responsibility for them. It's acknowledging our feelings to ourselves and our loved ones, and requesting what we need directly. Even hours or days after you acted out your feelings, you can say, "Wait. Let's press rewind. What I meant to say is ..."

Step Three:
Responding Differently

Compassion is like sunlight, awakening and
bringing joy to beings.
Its beauty is like a rainbow, lifting the hearts
of all who see it.
—TARTHANG TULKU

After we practice saying yes to what is, and witnessing our old habitual reactions, responding differently follows easily. It is a natural next step as we shift identities from our young ego self to our mature Being Self. All events in life begin to feel manageable to us, even the loss of a loved one.

One Saturday afternoon, seven days before the winter solstice, my mother's death felt imminent. She had been without food and fluids for too many days. As I lay in a hot bath with the room lit only by candlelight, I spoke to her spirit from my Being Self. I told her repeatedly that she was safe to surrender and let go into the light. Suddenly, I felt moved to get up and call my dear friend Debra, a meditation teacher at Spirit Rock Meditation Center. I asked if she would help my mother's spirit move toward the radiant light.

Debra had been anticipating my call and immediately dropped down into her Being Self. I was already in mine. "Imagine your mother at a time in her life when she was full of life," she said, "and picture her strong, healthy body in a beautiful sunny meadow. Now, because your mom was Lutheran, we'll bring the unconditional love to her through the great heart of Christ. So picture the radiant body of Christ walking toward your mother in the meadow. When he stands beside her, let his radiant light purify her body of all fear, shame, and guilt. Help her let go of her separate identity and melt into that radiant, bright, unconditional love of Christ." Before she hung up, Debra kept repeating, "Keep telling her spirit that she *deserves* unconditional love." My mother passed away a half hour after this meditation.

For any of us, whether facing death or moving through our everyday lives, feeling like we deserve unconditional love and really believing it

can be a huge stretch. Too often, declaring ourselves worthy of unconditional love calls forth images of a gigantic leap (a leap that we never
quite deserve). We think love is something we have to earn, something
others can take away if they disapprove of us. Few of us know that we
not only deserve unconditional love every moment but that we *are*, in
our heart of hearts, unconditional love and joy. Expanding and shifting into this unlimited love and joy in our Being Selves allows us to
respond differently to life. It makes it easy to embrace *all* our human
experiences with love and joy.

Responding differently is simply loving and accepting what is, including ourselves as we are. Not resisting. Not getting so caught up that we
forget who we are. If we feel sad, and don't want to feel sad, we love
our sadness *and* our not wanting to feel sad. If we feel lonely and hate
feeling lonely, we love ourselves for feeling lonely, and for hating feeling lonely. We accept it all. We hold *all* our feelings and thoughts in
love and joy. I first learned this concept years ago from Gay Hendricks.
It's incredibly freeing.

Responding differently means embracing *every* aspect of ourselves,
especially those places we rejected or hid from others. It means loving
our shame, our fear, our doubt and judgment, holding all these in compassion. It's a radical form of self-acceptance. It means loving even the
parts we tossed out as not good enough years ago. As Deepak Chopra
said, "To the knower inside, no amount of love or emotion can overwhelm it. All experience is direct." This kind of self-love takes practice,
day-to-day practice.

We have to know our old reactions well enough to laugh at ourselves, and take ourselves less seriously. We have to say yes so many
times to what makes us uncomfortable that we can notice what it feels
like *not* to resist life. This all takes time.

Transforming into Our Being Self

We tend to believe that people and things *out there* reject us, disappoint us, betray us, fail us in some way. But how we respond matters.
It matters a great deal to us and to how we experience life. *We* are the
ones resisting what is. *We* are the ones holding love and joy away. *We*
are the ones forgetting to respond from our compassionate Being Self.

So why were we conditioned to forget who we truly are?

As developing children, we saw ourselves as the center of the
Universe. In our undeveloped minds, every action revolved around us.
If Mom and Dad got divorced, we were sure it was our fault. If Dad

worked all the time and never spent time with us, we concluded we were not worthy of his attention. Inside, we decided we didn't matter. If Mom was depressed, drank too much, or cried often, we knew somehow we caused it. We thought, "If only I got better grades, or hadn't yelled, she'd be happy. Then she might pay attention to me." Our immaturity rendered us incapable of comprehending the whole picture.

As children, we are terrified of monsters and things that go bump in the night. That's part of childhood. We make sense of this adult world as best we can. Along the way, we slowly learn to hide our tender, vulnerable Being Selves—in order to survive, and be loved. The problem arises when these same immature beliefs that helped us survive and cope with overwhelming situations in childhood still remain intact years later, when we are adults. By now, we have bought into these beliefs for so many years that the mere thought of discarding them doesn't enter our mind. They sound like the truth.

For example, Louise believed in the *concept* of loving herself. In fact, she thought she did love herself. But her mind could not wrap around the crazy idea of loving her judgment and fear, the "bad" parts, as she called them. She had spent most of her adult life trying to get rid of her fear of abandonment that arose because her mother had given her up for adoption. She grew up believing love was earned, and people could take it away with disapproval.

Louise spent the first forty years of her life being rejected and blaming herself for failing at relationships. "If my own mother couldn't love me," she told me, "who could?" She worked hard in therapy to accept all parts of herself and respond differently.

The turning point came when she reclaimed all the rejecting thoughts she had projected onto lovers, friends, and strangers. "If I'm judging myself as unworthy—not all those people out there that I'm afraid are rejecting me—then I can change it," she exclaimed. "I could be busy telling myself that I do deserve love, that my needs are important." A few weeks later, after dropping her old belief, she found the world relating to her quite differently. "Friends are calling, inviting me for Christmas. Even this little elderly lady who never says hello acted superfriendly to me today. I like loving myself."

In order to respond differently, we need to perceive life from a different angle. To cultivate loving compassion, we need to stop responding from our young ego self. We need to question everything: our habitual reactions, our stories, our perceptions, and our beliefs. We need to throw right and wrong out the window. We need to expand into joy and love rather than shut down when something happens that we feel we can't handle.

From our Being Self, it's easy to respond to life with kindness and compassion. Easy to love *every* feeling, even shame and fear and guilt. Easy to see ourselves clearly, with compassion, without needing to hide the things we hold against ourselves anymore. Compassion makes it easy to hold life in unlimited joy. If we are the culprits, unconsciously telling ourselves we're not worthy, then why not respond differently? Why not tell ourselves we deserve unconditional love? Why not remind ourselves every hour that we are lovable and worthy, just for who we are? Why not reverse our past conditioning? Why not replace judgment and self-loathing with kindness and compassion? One of the most radical (and loving) things we can do is to hold *all* of our humanness in compassion.

Responding to Ourselves with Kindness and Compassion

It's not easy knowing ourselves, and loving ourselves, with compassion. It goes against common logic. "Easy" is repeating the same old reactions to doubt, fear, loneliness, and judgment that we've spent our whole lives refining. Easy is never questioning our reactions. Easy is buying into familiar stories. But easy creates more suffering.

For years now, we have trained ourselves to accentuate the positive and downplay negativity. For years, we used sheer willpower to reach goals far beyond our parents' wildest dreams. In every arena—techno-wizardry, fitness, climbing, flying, athletic prowess, travel, financial success, aging, and more—we have busted through so many former barriers that the Guinness book of records can't keep up. Whoever has the desire and financial means is now climbing the Himalayas. We took the late Joseph Campbell's advice and "followed our bliss" with a passion.

In this climate of new possibility, why on earth would anyone want to embrace fear, or shame, or doubt? Who would want to love these dark feelings? To our logical minds, it feels like sliding backward. But to our hearts, it's the next evolutionary step.

This step—bringing kindness and compassion to *all* parts of ourselves, especially those aspects we reject as bad and shameful—has the potential to change our human conditioning. It is not some quick behavioral fix to find happiness by doing one thing differently; it is a simple, courageous step that opens our hearts right in the midst of suffering. Not just when we feel safe, or comfortable, or happy, but all the time. As a therapist, I have cultivated compassion for years. But I recall one instance in my forties when my capacity for compassion took a leap. I knew, in my heart, that I had never fully forgiven how my mother's depression affected my childhood. Of course, I sent flowers on Mother's Day and her birthday. I called every Sunday, and we spent holidays together when possible. I had told her I forgave her, but it never felt completely genuine. I felt my heart hold back from fully loving her, or feeling her love. This all shifted when my close friend, a therapist, guided me through a lovingkindness practice.

When I called my friend, I was crying. But rather than just indulging my feelings, she asked me to sit on my meditation pillow. I closed my eyes and took some deep breaths. She asked me to hold the young me—that little girl who suffered so much terror as a child—in my belly, to pour compassion over her. As I engulfed the lonely, scared little me with compassion, I wept deeply. Next, my friend asked my Being Self to hold my depressed mother in my belly and pour compassion over the woman who was so depressed that she wanted to die. This time, I felt genuine compassion for my mother's predicament in a way I never had before. Later, I held my adult self in my belly and felt compassion for the young woman who entered adulthood with such deep scars. In the process, my heart opened wider. The love flowed again between my mother and me. I stopped needing my childhood to be any different than it was.

This step of loving even our resentment and shame, and loving those who hurt us, stretches us far beyond our lifelong loyalty to logic. When John came to a place in his therapy where it was time to love his shame, he balked. He understood working on his depression, which helped him identify and trust his feelings. But when I asked him to love the shame that was fueling his depression, he shook his head. "No way," he said. "I'm an educated man with strong principles. I was wrong to consent to sex with my babysitter, even if he was sixteen and I was eight."

"At eight years old, you didn't know what sex was. You just knew something was wrong. You complied because he threatened to tell your parents," I reminded him. "I'm asking if you would be willing, in your heart, to love that eight-year-old boy who was crazed with grief over losing his father, and love the shame you have carried in your body your whole life. Have compassion for that scared little boy. Stop holding it against yourself. Forgive. Would you be willing to love your shame, just as an experiment?"

"Yes," he agreed. "I'm willing to love my shame, though it makes no sense." He closed his eyes and held his eight-year-old self in compassion as he wept. That night, he told the woman he had been dating the story he had most dreaded telling anybody for fear of rejection—his molestation story. Soon after, he deepened his commitment to her.

Responding with kindness and compassion stretches our hearts. It moves us outside of our familiar comfort zone when we love every feeling, every fear, and every ounce of shame that hides deep inside us. It replaces harsh judgment with understanding, a tough lesson to embody. Not because we don't want to. But because we never learned how. We have few role models for this. Besides, in our heart of hearts, we don't feel we deserve it.

We human beings are funny. We possess these great hearts, overflowing with wisdom. Our Being Selves offer guidance daily through feelings, dreams, symptoms, intuitive hunches, and heartfelt longings. But instead of welcoming this inner guidance, we discredit uncomfortable feelings as "bad" and discard our longings as "silly" or "impractical." We never learned how to welcome them, listen to them, honor and respect them. Yet it's through honoring our inner guidance that the joy we so hunger for returns.

Responding to Others with Kindness and Compassion

As we find more compassion for ourselves, it's easier to respond to others with kindness and compassion. It just takes practice. Much of my work with couples involves teaching them how to stretch into their Being Selves when responding to their lover or spouse. Mostly, it involves dropping our personal agendas and habits of defending ourselves.

Recently, Connie and Frank came for a couple's session. Connie started to cry as she spoke. "I feel so tiny and vulnerable whenever I have feelings to share," she said. "If Frank yells loud or cusses, I disappear inside for weeks." I asked her if she was willing to tell Frank how scared and vulnerable this soft part of her felt. She nodded.

When I looked over at Frank, he appeared stiff and frozen. He was obviously scared of feelings, and scared of saying the wrong thing. I invited him to kneel in front of her. Between tears, Connie looked him in the eye and said, "I feel so terrified about sharing my feelings with you. This wounding happened at such a tender age in my life, preverbally, that I can't find any words when I need to share my needs and feelings."

Frank responded defensively, from his young ego self. "But when you told me I'm never there for you, and how I left a mess in the bedroom, I felt picked on."

Connie sighed a hopeless sigh. I shook my head. "Wrong response?" he asked.

"Try to be right here," I coaxed, "and really listen to what Connie just told you. She just taught you something very, very important about herself. Drop your personal agenda and be the biggest, most compassionate Being you can be right now. Respond from your heart with a simple phrase like, 'I hear you feel tiny and scared.' Reassure her scared, tiny toddler inside. Say, 'I'm here for you,' or, 'You're safe and you're loved.'"

Frank placed his hand over hers, and said verbatim what I had suggested. He repeated the words a second time. Connie's face softened. Her eyes lit up. She began to let in the tiniest possibility that he might be there for this scared, tiny, tender place in her. That night, lying in bed in the dark, their sharing had a softer, kinder, deeper quality. Over the next several weeks, she stopped hiding this part of herself from herself, and from him.

In the following session, he exposed *his* tender, scared self. "I just realized why I reject your feelings so," he said. "I've been scared my whole life of feeling inadequate. When you share your feelings, I feel picked on by you. It triggers my inadequacy. What I need is for you to preface your feelings with how much you love me."

How different our lives might be if we all responded to our fear and shame with compassion, and replaced our judgments with loving reassurance. "I hear you're afraid, honey, but I want you to know that you are safe and you are loved. I love you for feeling afraid, or ashamed, or despairing. I love you just as you are, in all your humanness." How different our relationships might be if we responded to our loved ones in this way. Imagine all the open space left over to create the life we want.

This starts by responding to ourselves with kindness and compassion. Not postponing or procrastinating over this new habit. This week a client asked, "How do you do it? How do you take someone as fearful and wounded as me and make me feel so happy?" I thought for a moment. "Lots of sweeping," I answered. "I help you sweep away all the fear, doubt, shame, and judgment that you learned to pile on top of yourself. What's left is your natural birthright, unlimited joy."

Practice Tools:

1. Set an intention this week to respond differently to situations. If you typically withdraw, push yourself to speak up. If you usually blow up in anger, declare a moratorium on your angry reactions and practice patience. However you typically react, try the opposite. Remember to *witness* your vulnerable feelings, blame-free, by talking about them rather than acting them out.

2. Practice shifting identities from your young ego self to your Being Self. When a feeling arises, lie on the floor or couch with a blanket over you, and take deep breaths in your belly. First notice any sensations in your arms, starting at your shoulders and moving down to your hands. Next, notice any sensations in your legs, moving from your hips to your feet. Then focus on your torso. Notice what feelings are present in your torso. Simply "watch" the feeling rather than identify with it, the way you might respond to a young child frightened by a dream. Be your mature Being Self reassuring your Inner Self when it's lost in fear, doubt, judgment, or shame. Be kind, compassionate, and loving without letting awareness be consumed by the feeling. Practice this throughout the day.

3. Give your Inner Self loving messages throughout the day. As many times as you think of it (at least once every hour), remind yourself that you are worthy and important, that you deserve unconditional love. Give yourself the same acceptance that a young child, puppy, or loyal dog gives you. Simple phrases such as, "I deserve loving compassion," "I am unconditional love," or "I am safe and wanted" are wonderful for the Inner Self to hear, as often as you think of it.

4. Plant compassion in your psyche and nurture it every day. Whenever you notice yourself feeling nervous, say inside yourself, "I love myself for feeling nervous." Whenever you find yourself avoiding fear, shame, or loneliness in yourself, respond with compassion. Try telling yourself, "I love myself for feeling shame, and I love myself for being afraid to feel the shame." Love is the most powerful healer. As we love all aspects of ourselves, we find it much easier to love all aspects of those around us. On New Year's Day, vow to your Beloved: "I commit to responding to you, and myself, with kindness, caring, and compassion all year."

Feeling Habits

It is the feeling level that controls
most of our inner life, yet often we are
truly unconscious of our feelings.
—JACK KORNFIELD

FEELINGS ARE RUDDERS. LIKE DREAMS, FEELINGS HELP GUIDE
us through the mystery of life. Yet to really hear them, we need to
unlearn some bad habits. We need to stop judging some as "good" and
others as "bad," and allow *all* feelings to flow through us, even the scary
ones. We need to stop ignoring the dark feelings until they make us ill
to get our attention. We need to stop losing perspective by getting so
caught up in them.

It's easy to make friends with feelings, once we set aside judgment,
doubt, and fear. Our egos want to distance us from our feelings by
thinking about and analyzing each feeling. But the quickest way back
to joy is to drop down into our bodies and feel our feelings directly.
Say yes to the feeling that is present, even if it makes you uncomfortable. Be curious. Imagine you are feeling disappointment, grief, or
loneliness for the first time. Note your habitual reaction to it, then let
it go. Welcome your new friend. Notice where you feel it in your body,
and its sensations. Ask it, "What are you trying to tell me?" Listen
respectfully to each feeling, the way you have always hoped someone
would honor you. Honor your feelings. Experiencing each feeling
directly, even the dark ones, is a gateway to joy.

Disappointment

*Although all of us desire happiness, few of us
reach that goal because of the seemingly endless
cycle of expectation and disappointment.*

—TARTHANG TULKU

Disappointment is such a bread-and-butter part of life. We eat, we sleep, we work, we get disappointed. As a child, small disappointments can feel devastating. But as adults, we expect ourselves not to flinch. "Get over it," we tell ourselves. "Grow up."

We feel disappointed when our expectations don't match reality. When we don't get what we want, or when we get what we tried to avoid. We have tiny disappointments every day—when a friend cancels dinner, the outdoor concert is rained out, or we get a cold. It's an integral part of life. And yet, we typically react in two ways: either we minimize our feelings, or we react in shock, as if it is never supposed to happen to *us*.

Disappointment is either no big deal or a huge deal, depending on how we react. When I'm working with a couple, and we wade through all the anger and resentment of the past several years, we often uncover a mishandled disappointment at the bottom of the broken trust. For example, Bill reluctantly agreed when the woman of his dreams—who had been his lover for some months—asked to stop being sexual until after the wedding. But deep inside, he stopped trusting her. Their sex life, and their marriage, never recovered. They divorced a few years later.

Alice withdrew emotionally for four years after her spouse failed to provide the emotional support she needed during a crisis. Monica left, even after her husband quit drinking, because of the disappointments she had endured during his ten years of drinking. Diane suffered years of chronic digestive pain after her husband talked her into moving out of state, then refused to find work. She felt forced to be the sole provider. Jane had an affair, but not until she had tried for years to get her husband to listen to her feelings. Her disappointment became unbearable.

I could go on. The point is, disappointments eventually destroy perfectly good relationships, if left unaddressed. It's not the fleeting disappointment but our holding onto past disappointments that does the destroying. If I dwell on the fact that you disappointed me, whether it happened last night or two decades ago, I stop seeing you with fresh eyes. My vision narrows. Spontaneity flies out the window. I anticipate more disappointment. I find fault with you, distance myself from you. And stop feeling joy.

These are all the ways our bodies have to act out our disappointment when we are unwilling to talk about it in healthy, nonblaming ways. As years go by, we build an entire belief system about "how you disappointed me" and "how you could do it again." But the entire belief system, no matter how logical, reasonable, and rational it sounds in our head, is cockeyed. What we really need to do is take responsibility for expressing our disappointment. Left unresolved, disappointments can plunge us into despair or hopelessness. They strongly affect our life choices, unconsciously. Most of us have experienced the painful disappointment of loving somebody who doesn't love us back. But even waking up with a cold can trigger disappointment. It doesn't take much.

The point is, we can choose joy, even amid disappointment. By *saying yes, witnessing,* and *responding differently,* we can hold the ordinary, predictable, everyday disappointments—and the major, life-changing ones, too—in compassionate joy.

Noticing Unconscious Reactions without Judgment

First, notice how you usually react to disappointment. See if you typically defend against it by believing you are "above disappointment," or if you treat it as if the sky is falling in. It's impossible to change your reaction unless you know what it is, fully. Invite it into your awareness *without judgment.* Welcome it. Be curious about it. Stop resisting or controlling it. Stop taking it so seriously. Expect it—don't act so shocked when it appears on your doorstep. The truth is, *when* you feel disappointed and *what* triggers it are completely out of your control. Acknowledge it, digest it, and move on.

Second, say yes to disappointment and witness your reactions. Notice how you react, inside, when you want to make love and your partner doesn't. Notice how you feel on Monday morning when the weekend is over and it's time to go back to work. Notice how you react to waking up with sniffles or a sore throat. Notice how you feel if a friend cancels something you were really looking forward to. Notice where you feel disappointment in your body. Try to describe the sensations of it to yourself: "I feel a pressure in my upper chest, or I feel punched in the belly." Notice, notice, notice.

Try treating yourself like a science project. Out of the many responses you could have in a given moment, notice what triggers disappointment in you. Welcome it into your awareness. Notice how long it lasts and which "stories" it generates. What feelings follow it? Just sit with the disappointment without having to minimize it or fix it or get rid of it. Now shift into your expanded Being Self, and hold the disappointment in loving compassion. Hold it in compassion the way you might hold a small child or pet who has been hurt. Practice letting joy share the same space with disappointment.

Disappointment, when not addressed, festers like poison. It raises havoc in our lives and our relationships. Over the years, it mutates into hot rage, cold resentment, or closed-hearted indifference. It eventually manifests as illness or chronic pain or worse.

Responding Differently to Disappointment

The third step is responding differently to disappointment. Rather than denying it or acting it out, it's important to acknowledge it—to ourselves first. And, when appropriate, to the person who triggered the disappointment. But not in a blaming way. Respond in that non-judgmental curious way, as if you are whispering inside yourself, "Hmmmmm, I'm feeling some disappointment right now. Interesting. I experience it as a collapsing of my chest. I wonder what triggered it." Welcome it as a good thing.

When you share this information with a loved one, express it from the *witness* position. Share it in a way that teaches the other person about your experience. Rather than blurting out, "You disappointed me!" in an angry tone, try saying, "When you said that, I felt disappointed. Here's where I feel it in my body. What I need from you now is . . ."

The moment you say yes to feeling disappointed and witness it, you shift identities. You let go of identifying with your young ego self, who takes disappointment so personally, and shift into your mature Being Self, who holds it all in love and joy. Sometimes the mere act of saying yes dissolves it. Other times, it becomes an opportunity to learn more about your habitual reaction to disappointment. In relationships, it can be a wonderful moment for healing, if you allow it. Here is an example:

Liz felt disgruntled with her marriage. Every week in therapy, she mentioned her desire for a divorce. She said she primarily stayed for the children. But as we explored her reasons for wanting a divorce, it came down to one huge disappointment ten years ago. One she had never forgiven her husband for. Liz became pregnant with their second child unexpectedly, after she and Ralph had agreed not to have any more children. Money was tight. One night, after they had drunk too much wine, Ralph begged her to have an abortion. Liz stormed out, refusing to discuss it again. She closed off her heart.

Now, ten years later, they have a wonderful son. Many times, Ralph has thanked Liz for keeping the baby and told her how much he loves their son. But Liz distanced herself emotionally. She criticized him daily. She convinced herself in her head that he was selfish, not the right man for her. After several urgings from me, she left therapy one afternoon agreeing to share her disappointment with Ralph. She was afraid he wouldn't even remember the incident, but she agreed anyway. At dinner that night, sitting in the back booth of a local café, she shared her painful disappointment. He listened. Tears streamed down her face. He held her and apologized for being so selfish. He said how much he loved their son. She never brought up divorce again.

We need to practice responding differently to disappointment. We need to see it as a gift, an opportunity to know ourselves better and create more closeness in our relationships. We need to experiment with letting it flow through us, unencumbered by resistance, denial, or blame. We need to stay present with the tender, vulnerable feeling.

Holding Disappointment in Compassion and Joy

We need to hold all of our feelings, even disappointment, in compassion and joy. Accepting it, embracing it just as it is, is the key. What does living in joy look like? Certainly not a life devoid of disappointment. It looks like "choosing joy," even now, even when I'm consumed with disappointment, even when I didn't get what I wanted. The question comes down to: "Am I brave enough, awake enough, desperate enough, fed up enough, to choose joy—even when I don't like my current experience, even when the person who loves me most in life just said something that devastated me? Even now?"

I don't mean living in a bubble. I mean acknowledging disappointment and holding it in joy and love. I mean being awake enough to see the disappointment train your mind has hopped on and holding even *that* in love and joy. I mean choosing joy *every* time you think of it. Not waiting. I mean being willing to feel disappointment directly, and choosing joy. Say, "I love myself for feeling disappointed, and I choose joy," then notice how it feels in your body. Don't force it. Just choose joy and see what happens. Watch your vision clear. Notice if choosing joy allows you to take the blinders off and really see who is standing in front of you, saying they love you (not your distorted image of them, filled with resentment and judgment). Breathe joy into your body right now, and notice what fresh thoughts enter your mind. Choose joy and see if that pain lessens. Experiment. How you respond to disappointment reverberates through your whole life.

Practice Tools:

1. Make a list of your major life disappointments. Pick the most devastating one. Spend ten minutes writing down how you reacted to it at the time, without any judgment about your reaction: If you were disappointed in yourself, did you guilt-trip, blame, shame, or hold it against yourself as a failure? Or did you respond with compassion, forgiving yourself? If it was in relation to another, did you shut down and stop trusting? Did you leave or resolve it? Did you withdraw into anger and cold resentment for years? Did you close your heart to that person and find it impossible to forgive him or her? However you reacted, hold your reaction in loving compassion. Create a ritual to let the disappointment go. You might write the whole incident on a piece of paper and burn the piece of paper as you vow to let it go. Or find a large stone that represents disappointment, and throw it in a lake, river, or ocean, letting the water carry it away.

2. Whether you formally meditate or just close your eyes for a few moments, move back in time to the very moment that disappointment first occurred. See how it feels in your body. Observe the story line that played in your mind, and see if it's a familiar story that plays whenever disappointment occurs. (Mind likes to attach our present disappointment to past disappointments and convince us that we aren't safe unless we obey the voice of fear and heed its warnings.)

3. For one week, make a commitment to express your disappointment whenever you notice it (without getting fired, of course). Even if you feel wimpy, even if you feel too vulnerable, even if it feels as if all you are saying every five minutes is, "I feel disappointed; I'm feeling disappointed; when you said that, I felt some disappointment . . . ," keep saying it anyway. Claim total responsibility for your disappointment by expressing it in a curious, nonjudgmental way, such as, "I felt disappointed when you said that, and I experience it as a

tightness in my diaphragm." Accept the feeling as it is. After all, from the perspective of our Being Self, disappointment is just a friendly visitor passing through, reminding us that we are human beings in bodies, inviting us to respond with compassion.

4. Whenever you feel disappointed, say yes to it. Allow it to be there. Watch it with curiosity. Imagine holding your disappointed Inner Self in compassionate love and joy, the way you might hold a young child who is frightened and needs reassurance. This is your mature Being Self witnessing the disappointment and responding differently, with kindness and loving compassion.

Discouragement

*If we can allow ourselves to feel
vulnerable and insecure when that is what
is arising, if we can be totally ourselves ...
we will find a great inner strength.*
—JOSEPH GOLDSTEIN AND JACK KORNFIELD

Discouragement is another feeling habit. We can count on it arriving on our doorstep from time to time, sometimes when we least suspect it. We can't control what triggers it, when it arrives, or how intense it gets. The thing we do have control over is how we respond.

Some people get discouraged about losing last weekend's golf tournament or taking fifth in the bike race they trained all year for. Others feel it when income slows to a trickle during a slow month, or when they fail to find resolution to a conflict right away. A friend of mine goes in and out of feeling discouraged that she hasn't won the lottery yet, even after playing for years.

Another friend for thirty years, who just turned seventy, feels very discouraged that she lost half her retirement in the post-9/11 stock market crash. We can feel discouraged when our lover, for the third night in a row, is too exhausted to make love. Or even more discouraged if we don't have a relationship at all. Feeling discouraged is normal. It comes in many flavors. What matters is whether we invite it in as an overnight guest, or turn it into a lifestyle. If we fail to see it clearly, discouragement can be the precursor to hopelessness, despair, or resentment. Like all life experiences, discouragement can be a gift, if we allow it. It's meant to protect us momentarily from risking more hurt while we lick our wounds and take a few days off to regroup. It's not meant to be a lifestyle.

When we deny our discouragement, or wallow in it far past its usefulness, it festers. Left to wreak havoc in our unconscious, it affects our choices, our perceptions, and our relationships for days, months, or even years. Since these human bodies arrived with feelings attached, we can count on feeling discouraged at times. Anything can trigger it, even things we thought would make us happy. But when we stay open and curious, nonjudgmental, we notice how it feels inside and listen to what it's asking of us.

Exaggerating and Talking about Discouragement

We've all experimented with painting gloom and doom across our foreheads, hoping somebody will ask, "What's wrong with you?" But this can take hours, even days. A much shorter path is to exaggerate our discouragement. By taking two minutes in our bedroom or other private space to indulge the "discouraged character" inside and say his or her thoughts out loud, we can usually find ourselves laughing before the two minutes are up.

For example, Beth thought about leaving her husband. Recently, she thought about it every day. In a couple's session, she finally told her husband how discouraged she had been feeling for months about not getting her needs met in their relationship. He reacted the way he always reacted at home. "Wait a minute," Bob said, holding his hand up to stop her. "I don't want to get stuck in some long, drawn-out discussion here."

Unfortunately for him, I was in the room to notice his resistance. Rather than let them argue about their stuck pattern in front of me, I said, "Stand up. Beth, you take this half of the room to exaggerate your pain. Pretend you're in drama class. This is your one opportunity to act out your fear and hopelessness to the hilt. Bob, you get this half of the room to resist Beth's feelings. Hold your hand up, say whatever you want to stop her from continuing. You both have two minutes. So give it all you've got. Ready, set, go."

Beth rounded her shoulders, tucked her head in like a turtle, and clasped her hands tightly to her chest, protecting her heart. "I want to tell you how sad and lonely I feel," she said in a young girl's voice, "but you always say 'No, don't be sad, don't feel that,' so I give up. Why bother. I've tried for five years, and you never allow my feelings. I've hit 'why bother' so many times, I skip right past it to thinking this will never work."

Meanwhile, in Bob's corner, he's waving his hands wildly in front of his face and chest to block Beth. "No, don't say that. Stop overwhelming me with all your feelings and ideas. Just let me work on my little projects in my little corner of the house, where I feel safe. Don't scare me with so many new things." They both broke out laughing.

By naming her discouragement, Beth was free to share her painful feelings underneath. She burst into tears, telling Bob how lonely she feels when he can't receive her feelings. Bob stroked her hair and held her close, a level of compassion he had never touched before because she had given up before she even exposed these tender feelings. At the end of the session, Bob agreed to drop his habit of resisting her feelings and, instead, say, "I hear you're feeling _____ and it scares me." To take responsibility for her part, Beth made a commitment to notice and *talk about* her discouragement with Bob rather than act it out. She also requested Bob to help her notice when she was acting it out.

It is our basic vulnerable needs—for nonsexual and sexual touch, for feeling listened to and heard, for appreciation and acknowledgment—that feel risky to express. We tend to give up on them way too soon. I encourage clients to ask for their needs fifty times before they even consider giving up. When we say yes to discouragement, witness our reaction, and respond differently, we teach loved ones about ourselves, and our needs, which creates more closeness. Our needs are our responsibility, not theirs.

Exaggeration takes two minutes. Noticing and talking about our discouragement takes ten or twenty minutes. Both are much shorter than staying unconscious and forcing our bodies to act it out, which can eat up days, weeks, months, or years.

Witnessing Discouragement and Responding Differently

Discouragement isn't picky. It arrives anytime, any place, at any age. We never really know when it will land in our lap. Any couple who has been struggling to get pregnant for more than six months knows well the roller-coaster ride from hopeful to discouraged that arrives with the cycles of the moon. We never know when the person we have committed our life to might suddenly stumble into a midlife crisis and fall in love with someone else. We might feel devastated when the child we doted on for eighteen years comes out as gay. Cancer victims reel with discouragement when first diagnosed, and keep reeling after several rounds of chemotherapy fail to destroy all the cancer cells.

Discouragement erodes our hope, sneers at our dreams, and carves a wedge between us and faith, if we let it. After a few tough blows in a row, it becomes more than just a fleeting feeling. It settles inside, sets up home, hangs pictures, and becomes a familiar way of perceiving the world. It becomes our reason to stop bothering to voice our needs, or even know what they are. After a devastating divorce or breakup, it clouds our joy and paints our future bitter black. Discouragement becomes a way of life.

Physical pain often triggers discouragement. After nine months of intense pain from a back injury, James agreed to surgery with one of the top five surgeons in the country. At twenty-five, he had his whole life ahead of him. Before surgery, the doctor told him that he would be running and playing soccer in six to eight weeks. James felt elated. After surgery, however, his pain intensified and he experienced a new, chronic pain in his back. His discouragement soon plummeted into depression.

"I don't care about soccer," he told me, "but why would he lie to me? I just want to be able to pick up my newborn baby when he arrives without dropping him." James felt more and more discouraged as he floated from doctor to specialist to physical therapist and found no answers for the pain he had lived with for the past year.

I invited him to stand up, walk around my office, and act out his discouragement. He shrugged. "Why bother?" he said. "I don't want to feel worse than I already do."

"Just try it," I coaxed. "See how you feel afterwards." After acting it out for a few minutes, he fell to his knees in grief. "I feel so lost and confused, Carolyn," he said. "I just want a normal life. I just want to work and make money and feel excited about my baby coming and take care of my pregnant wife."

"I know that's what you want," I replied, "but try saying yes to what is true. Focus directly on your pain and feel how much pain you are in. Really feel it."

He repeated his story instead. "What's true is that I injured my back a year and a half ago, I had surgery that didn't make the pain go away, and now I'm scared I'm stuck with this horrible pain, and feeling spaced out on painkillers, the rest of my life."

"Yes," I agreed, "I hear how scared you are. In this moment, drop down into your fear. Really feel how scared you are. Locate the fear in your body. Breathe into it."

As he focused directly on his fear and acknowledged it fully, it lessened. As he breathed in his belly and focused directly on his back pain, it began to soften and feel less intense. At home, James began developing his own relationship with his pain. Rather than popping a pain pill every time it flared up, he would pause, breathe into his pain, feel it, and ask, "What is it? What are you trying to tell me?" Instead of getting angry at it, he learned to say, "I love myself for feeling pain, and I love myself for hating having pain right now." Though he is still healing, he has replaced discouragement with compassion.

James started college, something he never believed he could do prior to his injury. James learned to respond differently to his pain and to life, more differently than he ever imagined.

Discouraged to Be Who I Am on a Soul Level

Deep inside, in our unconscious, there rests a layer of discouragement that few of us realize is there. It seeps into our lives so early in life, so soon after we are born, that it doesn't feel like discouragement at all. After years of sharing the same body with it, it just feels like part of us. It's as familiar as our arms, legs, and the shape of our noses. But it's discouragement. It's a deep, dark, underbelly layer of discouragement that comes from never being seen or heard for who we truly are.

As children, when our Being Self was never seen or heard by our parents (who never knew a Being Self even existed), we buried any awareness of our essential self deep inside. To keep it safe, we forgot about it. We had to, because part of being young is that we are dependent on parents and teachers for our survival. We learn quickly to do anything we have to for love, including hide our feelings, swallow our tears, stifle our anger, and perform well. Anything less than this is too painful. Long before adulthood, we identify ourselves with what we think, feel, and believe. We, too, forget our Being Self exists. We just notice a restlessness and dissatisfaction with life that won't go away.

When we fall in love, this is reinforced, if our lover or spouse is also incapable of fully seeing and hearing who we truly are. So we get divorced, fall in love again, and, a few years later, feel discouraged *again* that who we truly are is not heard or seen. We entertain our worst fear, that maybe we really aren't lovable at all. After a while, we give up. We settle for this gnawing, empty feeling in our bellies as "just the way life is."

That is why it's so critical to touch this deep layer of discouragement, to make it conscious. The problem is never that we are not worthy of love. The problem is that we are looking in the wrong places. We are looking *outside* to others for something we need to first give ourselves. Once we reach adulthood, we have to be the first in line to connect with our Being Selves, to see and hear who we truly are. We are the ones who reassure our soft, vulnerable Inner Selves when they tenderly ask, "Am I safe to be exactly who I am in this physical body? In this love relationship? In this world?"

We are afraid to ask. Afraid to look inside. Afraid to dredge up this longing that was safely tucked away so long ago. In this outer-oriented culture with techno-wizardry grabbing our attention at every corner, it takes effort to explore our inner world. It requires time, attention, faith, and trust. It takes effort to come to know ourselves, and love ourselves, at this deep level. It takes time to sit quietly with ourselves and ask, "Who am I?" again and again, until our hearts finally trust us enough to respond. It takes time to patiently wait for the answer from our Inner Self, which has been so ignored for so many years by everyone (including ourselves) that it's hard for it to trust anyone.

It takes time and patience to practice meeting life with our vulnerability and with our hearts wide open. Time to recognize our knee-jerk reactions to discouragement and let them go. Time to fall on our faces and get up again, consciously. Time to witness our feelings without habitually buying into them. Time to face a broken heart fully awake and find the courage to open to love again. Time to open our hearts— not just when it's safe but right now, in the middle of back pain, discouragement, hopelessness, loss, and illness. In other words, it takes time, patience, attention, and commitment to develop a relationship, a solid compassionate friendship, with our tender Inner Selves.

Acknowledge the Possibility of Deep Discouragement

This level of discouragement, not being seen or heard for who we truly are at such a tender age, is difficult to touch at first. It's important to be open and curious, to wonder, "How did I react when my parents weren't able to fully see and hear who I am?" By asking and listening to our hearts and bellies, we can reconnect with our deepest core.

One thing I do with new clients, as soon as they seem ready, is have them lie down on my soft futon, close their eyes, and take deep breaths into their belly. I ask them to "presence" in their bodies by dropping their awareness down into their body and seeing whatever they notice. Often people respond with, "I don't feel anything" or, "I feel good." (We are well trained to live in our heads and discount our body sensations and feelings as annoyances to get rid of with the latest pill.) However, as we reconnect with our bodies, feelings, and intuition, we are rewiring a direct path to our core Being Self.

Encouraging Ourselves to Be Who We Truly Are

Seeing, hearing, and loving ourselves just as we are is the shortest path to joy. Too often, we are afraid to look inside, afraid to face the emptiness and self-hatred we fear we might find. But we can love even the fear, even the emptiness and self-loathing. That is how we tell our spirits that it's safe to be who we are in these bodies. Loving all of it. Loving the discouragement, even if we can't feel it. Loving the depression, despair, hopelessness, and helplessness. Loving all of what it is to be in a human body. That is responding differently. That is bringing compassion to who we are as human beings in human bodies. That is breaking the cycle of not feeling seen or heard that has been passed down by our ancestors for generations.

The next time your tender heart gingerly asks, "Am I safe to be fully who I am in my body, in this world?" answer a resounding, "Yes! Yes! Yes!" Begin now seeing and hearing who you truly are, being the best friend your Inner Self could ever hope for.

Practice Tools:

1. Sit down for ten minutes and list ten or twenty discouragements you have lived through in your life. Simply acknowledging your discouragement, big or small, is a quick way to say yes to it. Sometimes the only thing your Inner Self needs to let it go, is simply acknowledgment. Then pick one especially painful moment of discouragement, and take five minutes to write what you learned from it. Write about the "gift" of the experience.

2. Pick something you feel mildly (or wildly) discouraged about in your life. Find a private room at home, or lock the door of your office, and take two minutes to exaggerate this feeling. You may feel discouraged that nobody cares about your feelings. Or still discouraged that you didn't get that promotion last year. No matter what it is, indulge it for two full minutes. Before the two minutes are up, you may laugh heartily and feel much lighter.

3. Pick one week to witness your habitual reaction to discouragement. Be curious, without judgment. Notice your reaction. Do you deny feeling discouraged? Milk it to the last drop? Sulk for hours or days? Withdraw emotionally? Get even more curious by noticing what triggers it and which stories it generates. Notice how it feels in your body. Which feelings follow it? How soft or loud does it sound inside? Just notice, without needing to change or fix it. Notice if it stops you from taking risks, or talks you out of your needs and wants. By witnessing it, you free yourself to respond quite differently.

4. Make a commitment to *talk about* your discouragement with your spouse, lover, or friend next time it arises. Rather than buying into it, practice speaking about it from the witnessing perspective, with compassion. That is, say, "I notice when you said that, I felt discouraged inside, like, 'why bother asking you to listen to me?' But I want to say it anyway. What I need right now is . . ."

Making Friends with . . .

Angst

When you return to your Self,
this is called awakening . . . freedom.
—H. W. L. POONJA

Sheila, a woman in her late forties who normally has a great sense of humor, arrived in my office on the verge of tears last week. "I'm nothing but a lazy procrastinator," Sheila said, shaking her head. "I never do anything right. And now, thanks to therapy, I have to take full responsibility for all the messes I create. Before, I could at least blame somebody else."

"Just tell me what happened," I suggested in my best comforting tone.

"I blew it, again. I should have taken care of it months ago," she continued. "But no, not me, I wait until the last minute, until a crisis comes, and then I finally kick in." Judging herself is a deeply entrenched habit she's been working on. But she didn't recognize it this time. She was immersed in it. "This morning, my south pasture was flooded from an irrigation leak. A crisis I could have avoided if I'd just maintained the irrigation system the way Fred told me to when he installed it last fall. But not me . . ."

"Tell me exactly what happened, Sheila," I prodded.

"What happened is I messed up *again*," she yelled. "I failed to do what I was advised to do. And now my baby lambs and goats can't eat because their food is under water!"

"Sheila, tell me exactly what happened without judging yourself."

She paused and furrowed her brow, as if caught with her hand in the cookie jar. "My irrigation system got a leak in the night," she spoke slowly, careful to leave out any self-blame. "My south pasture is flooded. I called Fred this morning, and he's fixing it now." She breathed a sigh, finally free of the angst she had judged herself with for hours.

I love the word "angst." I fell in love with the word at a Vipassana meditation retreat in San Rafael, California. In 1992, James Baraz and Carol Wilson were teaching a seven-day retreat. During an evening dharma talk (a forty-five-minute teaching on Buddhism), Carol Wilson taught us about angst. She described angst as the way we tend to *embellish* our experiences with stories, blame, and judgment. For the next several days, I watched my mind create angst. I noticed soreness in my left knee and watched my thoughts jump to, "Knee injury! Possible surgery! Meditation isn't healthy for me! How will I ever fit surgery into my busy schedule?" I watched my mind leap from the slightest twinge of discomfort to monstrous fears in two seconds, complete with elaborate stories to worry and fret over and totally consume my awareness.

Angst is everything we pile on top of *what actually happened*—the judgments, doubts, fears, stories, memories, and fantasies we add to "what is." Webster's dictionary defines angst as "a feeling of anxiety." But my years of consciousness training and working with clients have taught me that angst is much more than that. Angst covers the 90 percent of embellished story that we fondly call "life."

Bare Attention Takes Conscious Effort

Buddhists have a great term for sticking with the facts. They call it "bare attention." Bare attention is being present with what is, period. It's standing in the present moment with fresh eyes, an open heart, and an empty mind. No expectations. No judgments. No preconceived notions. No agendas. It's showing up in each moment brand-new.

In 1976, Joseph Goldstein, cofounder of the Insight Meditation Society (IMS), a meditation center in Barre, Massachusetts, explained in his book, *The Experience of Insight*: "Bare attention means observing things as they are, without choosing, without comparing, without evaluating, without laying our projections and expectations on to what is happening." And, as Buddhists fondly teach in dharma talks, "This could take a lifetime."

In contrast, most of us tend to be "kitchen-sink" communicators. Inside our own minds, we throw all sorts of judgments, blame, righteous indignation, preconceived notions, and story lines into the way we perceive "just the facts." With the people we love most, the ones we see every day, we achieve ever greater heights of "kitchen-sink" communiqués, especially if we're angry, disappointed, afraid, or having a bad hair day.

Instead of saying, "My husband went to the fitness center for a couple of hours, and it's triggering some lonely feelings in me," we tell our friend, "He left without kissing me goodbye or anything. And I never know how long he's going to be gone. For all I know, he's going to see some woman from work. I'm so lonely, I just don't know if we'll make it. Someday, I won't be here when he gets home, and then he'll regret it."

We never learned how to "presence" our feelings. We never learned to say, "I'm noticing some sadness in my chest right now. It bubbled up after we made love, babe. Can you hold me while I let these tears come?" We avoid asking directly for what we want, or need, in such a tender moment, because we fear rejection, or not feeling heard.

Instead we communicate defensively, manipulatively, seductively, bracing ourselves for disappointment, creating angst by how we ask. If we do speak up (which means overcoming the notion that tears don't fit with hot sex, or even not-such-hot sex), we blurt out, "You're never there for me! Why can't you be there for me?"

Unconsciously, we create an argument, extinguishing the tender feelings, convincing ourselves that nobody cares. Next time, we will probably jump right past voicing our tender needs at all and move directly into fear and resentment. Or we can recognize our part in creating the situation, witness our feelings, and press rewind. "Wait. That's not what I meant to say. What I really want is to ask you to . . ."

Identifying Angst

Beliefs love nothing better than to prove themselves right, again and again. Such childhood beliefs as, "nobody cares about my needs" or, "I can't trust anyone with my tender feelings" gain strength as our angst runs wild. When we identify the angst we make up in our heads—based on judgments, expectations, preconceived ideas, and misperceptions—we stop reinforcing negative core beliefs. Very simply, angst creates more angst. The best antidote is to take responsibility for recognizing your needs, and state them specifically.

How We Create Angst and How to Stop Ourselves

Once we get the hang of witnessing all the ways we embellish situations, it can be quite entertaining. And insightful. But we have to be willing to laugh at ourselves.

One morning last fall, I was swimming in great angst without any awareness of it. After my mother entered a nursing home three years ago, I took over handling her bills. When I called the billing department at the nursing home, Ellen explained that my mother's account was behind $850 and that her private pay portion had gone up from $1,155 per month to $1,166 per month. That's the bare facts. My anger was the angst I imported. All my guilt about leaving my mother in a nursing home, and my rage built up from the past thirty years over skyrocketing medical costs, exploded inside me. I lost it.

To witness myself, I sat down to meditate on what had just happened. I inquired inside, "Where do I feel the anger in my body? What does it feel like? Who suffers when I explode?" I do, and the people around me. My blood pressure rises. My heart races. I lose all sense of inner peace. The joy I woke up with flies out the window.

In my silence, I peeked underneath the anger to touch my grief and frustration. I live thousands of miles away from my mother at 7,500 feet, an elevation she can't tolerate at eighty-two years of age. Her nursing needs are beyond my abilities. She is dying, and I'm spending her last precious moments on the phone with Medicaid and Medicare.

Anger is easy. It requires no vulnerability on our part. It's our cohort when we take life too personally. It's fear gluing this present moment to some past disappointment and convincing us to play it safe, at all costs. It's the pain we bring to what is and then blame someone else for. It's our willingness to get so immersed in what sits on our front burner that we completely forget to hold *even this* pain or discomfort in love and joy. It's getting lost in things that won't really matter tomorrow, or next week, or next year.

When we take ourselves too seriously, angst jumps in and takes us for a long ride, until we say stop. A bright man in his fifties came to me depressed. The week before, he had driven himself to a mountaintop to kill himself. Fortunately, a family with two small children drove up to the same mountaintop and parked right beside him. Bill loves children. In fact, he was down in the dumps because his son had refused to let his grandson visit for a week because he had been depressed lately. He looked at the children in the car, thought about his grandson, and drove home in time for dinner.

When he related the story to me, he laughed at his crazy thinking, the angst that had almost talked him into killing himself. Several months later, Bill hugged me goodbye, a much happier man. He was finally doing what he had dreamed about for years—moving to Oregon and starting his own consulting business.

Wrapping Our Angst in Loving Joy

The choice is ours. We can embellish our hurt, disappointment, and pain in angst when they appear on our doorstep, or focus on just the bare facts. We can take our lover's feedback personally, or silently witness our reactions inside while receiving their truth.

The operative word is *choice*. When we make our old patterns conscious, when we pause to acknowledge our feelings, we can respond differently. We can choose joy, even now. Then we can cultivate bare attention. We can say yes to what is, witness what is *and* the angst we bring to it, and free ourselves to respond differently.

No matter what phone calls come in, what curve balls are thrown our way, what our wild teenagers are up to today, we can surround all of it with loving compassion, humor, and inner joy. Practice reminding yourself, "I choose joy, even now."

Practice Tools:

1. Set an intention to *see* angst. Get familiar with what it looks like, sounds like, and feels like. Every morning for a few weeks, whisper to yourself, "I'm willing to notice any angst I bring to what happens today." Repeat it five times to yourself, then go about your day. Let yourself be entertained by the judgments, stories, expectations, or fearful beliefs that wrap around the bare facts. Then choose joy.

2. Cultivate bare attention. Practice telling yourself exactly what happened, free of embellishment. Witness judgments, doubts, and expectations without buying into them: "We made love last night. I felt tired. I noticed some judgment that I shouldn't be tired. I loved myself for feeling tired and for judging myself. When I told my lover how I felt, we shifted gears, caressed each other, and made slow, gentle love. The next morning, I heard this voice of judgment again, this time telling me that I ruined our lovemaking. I labeled it and let it go. I chose joy in the present instead."

3. Angst works in collusion with the "not good enough" belief buried deep inside. Notice whenever angst tries to make your cold, your work, your relationship, your current experience, and your efforts as a loving human being not good enough. Say yes to it, label it "angst," and let it go. Respond to the tender feelings inside—the hurt, disappointment, fear, sadness, or loneliness—with reassurance and gentle compassion. Choose joy in each moment.

Making Friends with . . .
Loneliness

A major turnaround point in our lives
comes when we become willing to experience.
Then we can begin to feel joy and passion.
—GAY HENDRICKS

Loneliness is like winter. We anticipate both with a certain level of horrific dread. Long dark nights, short cold days, far too much quiet time for reading and introspection. Nobody raises their hand and volunteers to feel lonely. We brace ourselves against it, sometimes for our whole lives. But when it's all over, when the spring thaw arrives, we look back on that time as a gift of wisdom, a rare gift that is hard to put into words.

We dread loneliness. We'll do anything to avoid it—put up with boredom, pain, years of unhappiness, even affairs. Some of us marry someone we don't love just to bypass loneliness. We stay in bad relationships long after they have soured and died to avoid feeling lonely. We withhold our deepest needs and feelings for fear that the other person might leave—and leave us alone. We indulge our insatiable cravings for food, sex, drugs, alcohol, exercise, or surfing the net to avoid feeling lonely. The entertainment business thrives on our desperate need to avoid that gnawing feeling in our bellies.

But what is it we dread so? What if we brought curiosity and openness to our fear of loneliness? What if we said yes to even this? What might we learn about ourselves, about loneliness, about being human? Like sadness, confusion, frustration, or fear, loneliness is one more feeling that comes with the turf of being human.

We can't avoid it. We can be settled into a loving, nurturing relationship and still feel lonely. We can be single or married, young or old, healthy or ill, and still be lonely. Everything can be going great in our life—work, love, family, health, friends—and loneliness still strikes. So if avoiding it doesn't work, what does?

Becoming Good Friends with Loneliness

Loneliness lives at a much deeper level than whether we have a lover right now or not. In fact, it has little to do with "out there" and who happens to be loving us, or rejecting us, in this moment, though that can trigger it. Loneliness comes from *us abandoning ourselves*. It comes from us not acknowledging our needs and feelings, and not voicing them.

As with most fears, the first step is to turn and face our loneliness. Acknowledge it. Say yes to feeling lonely. Hang out with it in meditative silence. Feel the *energy* of it underneath the story filling your mind. Get to know it better, like a friend. Invite wisdom into your awareness by asking yourself, "What triggered this feeling? Where do I feel it in my body? Underneath the label of loneliness, how would I describe this feeling to my best friend? What thoughts or story lines does it trigger?" By witnessing loneliness, we instantly recognize that who we are, in our core, is much bigger and more expanded than the contracted feeling of loneliness itself. We hold it in loving compassion.

Loneliness Signals Us to Honor Our Needs

Loneliness comes when we are disconnected from ourselves. When we have not been paying enough attention to ourselves. When we have been sweeping our feelings under the rug, postponing our needs for "more important causes." In other words, when we have stepped out of integrity with ourselves.

Loneliness gnaws at our insides, warning us that things have gone awry, no matter how much alcohol we drink to numb it, or how many pain meds we take to kill the pain. It asks us to feel heard and seen— not by some hot new lover or old friend, but by ourselves. It demands that we get to know ourselves better. It comes when we are not listening to our needs, not honoring our feelings, not connecting with our Inner Self. It bugs us like a pesky fly until we finally listen. It's our job to pay attention.

Lori called me at two o'clock on Sunday afternoon. Sunday was the day she wasn't preoccupied with work, the day she really wanted a drink to numb the pangs of loneliness. She called me instead. I scheduled an appointment with her the next day.

"I'm so lonely," she blurted out before even sitting down. "This stupid fibromyalgia limits me so much that I isolate at home. I don't want to socialize. Why would I want to spend my Saturday night watching others eat and drink whatever the hell they want? I'm sick of feeling deprived, sick of Swiss chard and rice, sick of having to be so particular at the grocery store, and so narrow in my choices for dinner." She took both fists and pulled at her hair in frustration.

"You sound angry," I reflected. I asked her to spend two minutes hitting a large pillow to release her anger and frustration. She did. Then I invited her to stand in front of the full-length mirror in my office and say out loud what she told her Inner Self routinely. She furrowed her brow at me with a quizzical look. I said, "Your body has required special diet needs the past two years. How do you typically respond to that?"

"Oh, I hate it," she insisted.

"So look at yourself in the mirror, look directly into your eyes, and tell that beautiful woman what you usually say to her about her special needs," I offered.

She took a deep breath. "I hate you! I hate you for depriving me of a normal life," she said softly, embarrassed to treat herself this way in front of a witness. "I stick by your stupid strict diet for a few days, then I have to eat a bag of chips, or chocolate, and I cycle downhill into low energy and feeling sick again. I'm sick of telling my husband my latest symptoms. And he's sick of hearing them. I'm surprised he hasn't left."

When our Inner Selves, in pain, need our attention, we tell ourselves the cruelest things without even realizing it. Lori began to cry when she heard herself out loud.

"If I was your Inner Self, struggling with this disease," I said, "I might feel lonely too, given how you are treating me. You don't know how long this disease will last, but you have learned over two years of trial and error that exercise gives you more elbow room diet-wise, and that eating certain foods makes you feel better. I invite you right now to close your eyes and ask your Inner Self what she would like to hear from you."

Lori closed her eyes and asked her heart what would sound good. "She'd like to hear that I love her," she said, "and that I'm here for her. She needs reassurance that we can handle this, together," she said. "I'm willing to love my disease unconditionally." She replaced resistance with acceptance, taking fifteen minutes each day to close her eyes and connect with her inner feelings, needs, and longings.

Whether we face diabetes, chronic pain, alcoholism, or cancer, it's common to feel lonely. It's not the disease that causes the loneliness, though. It's our isolation, our self-judgment, and our inability to still love ourselves despite the cards life has dealt us. Lori's fibromyalgia hasn't gone away. It may never. But her symptoms eased when she listened to her Inner Self and responded differently, with compassion.

Taking Full Responsibility for Our Loneliness

The way to alleviate loneliness is not to rush out and find a new lover, and another, and another. It's taking full responsibility for acknowledging it. Turning and facing it. It's not placing the huge responsibility of whether we're lovable on someone else. It's loving and supporting ourselves. Since we never learned how to love well, period, it's being open to learning how. It's being kinder, substituting loving compassion for self-hatred. It's making friends with ourselves. It's loving ourselves for feeling lonely.

When a client says he or she feels lonely, I often say, "Good. Really feel it. Focus directly on it. Really feel how lonely you feel." This welcomes loneliness as simply a red flag reminding us that we have abandoned ourselves.

Loneliness pushes us past a broken heart, past hiding in some dark corner licking our wounds. It pushes us into going on a ridiculous blind date that changes our lives. It forces us to connect—with our own heart, and with the world. It teaches us to see and hear ourselves before we can fathom teaching others how to see and hear us. Loneliness is a gift, if only we recognize it. If only we invite it inside for a cup of tea and a chat.

Practice Tools:

1. Grab a notebook, find a quiet place to sit alone for thirty minutes, and list some times you felt lonely in your life. Pick the worst one. Take twenty minutes to write about your loneliness and the wisdom it taught you about yourself and life.

2. Take five minutes to complete this sentence over and over: "As long as I do _____, I avoid feeling lonely." (This might include getting stoned, overindulging in bread or chocolate or caffeine, reaching for a beer or glass of wine, surfing the net, jumping immediately into a new relationship, or working all the time.) Be completely honest with yourself. Amuse yourself with all the ways you have manufactured to skip over, crawl under, or bypass loneliness. Now ask yourself, "Does it work? Does it just postpone the inevitable? What price do I pay for this in my health, my relationship, my creative expression?"

3. Next time loneliness lands in your lap, create some open time to get to know it. Close your eyes, take some deep breaths, and ask your higher wisdom: "What triggered my loneliness? How does it feel in

my body? What past memories feed it? What stories does it trigger? What feelings come with it, or follow it?" Do some journaling about it. To access your higher wisdom, just ask the question, take deep breaths, and patiently wait for whatever bubbles up. Once you start to make friends with loneliness, it will never seem as dreadfully scary again.

Making Friends with . . .

Sadness and Grief

Joy is something entirely
different from pleasure.
—KRISHNAMURTI

As I was writing this book, my stepmother died of cancer. I found
out the afternoon of my fifty-fourth birthday, while I was on
vacation on Maui. That evening, I sat in the outdoor hot tub sobbing.
My eyes were glued to the red planet Mars as it hung in the black,
moonless sky, just as it had every evening that summer. Its presence
reassured me that the sky wasn't falling in.

I felt Dorothy's spirit hovering nearby. In between sobs, I spoke to
her: "I want you to answer the phone one more time, Dorothy. I want
to say 'I love you' once more and hear you say back, 'I love you, too,
Carolyn.' I want more moments to tease you, to laugh with you, to
share family gossip with you. I just want more." I spent that evening
and the next few days reviewing all the wonderful, funny times we had
spent together, thanking her for loving my dad for thirty years and for
welcoming me into her life, too.

After some days, grief gave way to a renewed joy of life. I felt energized, very awake and present. On my morning jaunt to the outdoor
hot tub, I paused to breathe in the fragrant kahili ginger growing wild
in my friends' backyard. While resting silently in the hot tub, I heard
the soft flap of doves' wings overhead. On a morning walk, I slowed
down to drink in the purple and pink bougainvillea lining the road.

I chuckled to myself, remembering my visit to Dad and Dorothy's
place last May. The first thing I woke to each morning was Dorothy
puttering in her kitchen, making coffee so she and Dad could read the
morning paper in bed. I recalled sitting on the living room floor, pack-
ing my mother's china to ship home. I began humming the tune of
"Do-Re-Mi" from *The Sound of Music*, which I first learned as a young
girl. Dorothy sat in her blue, worn-out recliner and joined in, humming along with me. That moment I will treasure forever.

We had all shared a good laugh the night before when she stuck a
cube of butter in the oven to soften it and forgot about it. The chemo
had destroyed her memory. Every morning she burned something—

the toast, the oatmeal, my brown rice. And yet she still insisted on cooking for my dad and me. When I got short with her about burning my brown rice, she muttered, "We'll see how good you do at eighty-four after several rounds of chemo!" I apologized. We hugged. Now all those bungled moments are precious, irreplaceable memories. I want more.

Suddenly, that Buddhist saying about holding the ten thousand sorrows and ten thousand joys of life in our great hearts took on deeper meaning. I felt my own heart stretching and expanding as it struggled to hold my grief, and my joy, all at the same time.

Carving Out Space for Hidden Sadness

It's easy to connect the dots between losing a loved one, or suffering through a difficult divorce, and grief. We all give ourselves permission to cry then. But what about the unacknowledged sadness we carry in our bellies and our hearts? I've never met a man or woman in my practice who wasn't carrying some sadness inside, sadness they had long ago forgotten. I first see it in the lackluster, vacant look in their eyes. I first hear it in the lackluster way they talk about their needs and feelings. But mostly it's the chronic pain and symptoms of our bodies that point exactly to the place where we carry our sadness inside. And it's our bodies where the healing needs to take place.

Sometimes, for no apparent reason, sadness wells up in the middle of lovemaking, when we are vulnerable and naked. But we stuff it back down, believing it will "ruin the mood." Other times, we get mad at ourselves for bursting into tears on our way home from work. Or it wells up unannounced when we are sick at home for a day, free from the fast-paced busyness. We get mad when there is no obvious reason for feeling sad, or it's interrupting our plan. But the truth is, asking, "Why am I sad?" gets us nowhere, except out of our bodies and into our heads. It cuts us off from our feelings. And sadness is meant to help us to connect with our needs and feelings, to pay attention to our Inner Selves. Especially in midlife, whatever pain and sorrow we have not addressed demands our attention. Welcoming our sadness, surrendering into it, allowing it to flow through us, connects us with our deepest truth, and our heartfelt longings.

Cindy came to see me after having an abnormal pap smear. She was petrified of cancer, but the next checkup wasn't for three months. I explained to her that our bodies develop symptoms in exactly the areas where we are carrying unexpressed feelings.

I had her lie down on my futon and close her eyes. I invited her to breathe deeply in her belly and focus her awareness directly on her pelvic area. "Now imagine sending each exhale directly down into your uterus. Listen for any memories, feelings, or images to bubble up." She breathed in silence for a long time. Suddenly, she burst into tears. "I'm remembering my abortion," she said. "It feels as if it happened yesterday, even though it was twenty years ago." I encouraged her to really feel how sad she felt.

She grieved for several minutes. Then she felt guided by her inner wisdom to speak to the spirit of the aborted child. "I'm so sorry I couldn't give birth to you. I had no money. The father was abusive to me, and I desperately had to get out of that relationship. I wanted you. I loved you. I just couldn't." She sobbed more. Toward the end of the session, she forgave herself. Her eyes looked radiant. Three months later, when she went back for her next checkup, her pap smear was normal.

Facing Our Sadness is the Short Path to Joy

Unexpressed sadness often crops up in our awareness as blaming stories, resentments, irritability, restlessness, or illness. Sometimes, in quiet moments, we may feel an empty hole in our chest, but we quickly distract ourselves. Other times, festering sadness feeds the anger that we unleash behind closed doors. Often we believe we already worked through past hurts over being molested, or abandoned, or betrayed. But our bodies give the final verdict, the true verdict. It's up to us to listen to our bellies and our hearts by saying yes to sadness, even if it looks endless at the starting gate. It's up to us to create a safe container for our souls to express themselves. As we respond with compassion to sadness, we welcome it as a red flag guiding us to our deepest longings.

Trusting Our Own Tears Enough to Listen to Them

If we sit on our sadness, postponing it until some more convenient time that never comes, we sit on our joy, too. Holding any feeling away from our awareness holds all feelings away, including love and joy. By setting aside time, and setting an intention such as, "I'm willing to feel whatever sadness I've been unwilling to feel," we can let our sadness flow. As we respond with loving compassion to the years of sadness and grief we have buried deep inside, we let our grief be a gateway to the unlimited joy in our hearts.

When Jane's mother passed away suddenly of a heart attack, Jane wanted to die too. She called me, frightened because she couldn't find any reason to live. She was turning sixty shortly, her children were grown, and she couldn't find the right man to love. Finally, when Jane breathed into the sadness in her heart, she wept like a baby. She let herself feel how much she had loved her mother, despite their differences.

"I miss talking to her on the phone twice a week, getting her input," she said.

"Breathe right into that sadness, Jane," I encouraged. "Really feel how sad you are." She spent the entire hour crying and talking about her mother. And the next two sessions. A few months later, she called to tell me, "I found a good reason to live, Carolyn. I bought a hundred acres with my inheritance, and I'm inviting community members to participate in an organic garden."

We can't control what life hands us. But we can respond with respect, compassion, and kindness. We can honor our sadness without needing to know why. We can sit with the deep grief that arises when our Being Self finally feels seen and heard for who we truly are.

Sadness and grief are natural, normal, necessary parts of life. All they need is to be acknowledged and expressed. Sadness guides us down into our bellies and reconnects us with our deepest truth. When we cry, we finally let ourselves say the soul truth we have been too petrified to speak before to loved ones.

As I swam with four dolphins off Maui shores the day after Dorothy died, I was flooded with memories of her countless oil paintings of flowers, nature, and landscapes. "Life is filled with so many joyful moments," she often reminded me. "You just have to look for it."

Sadness is a precious gift. It forms the river to carry us forward into whatever's next in our lives. It tells us immediately, irrevocably, what is really important to us. It brings us closer to ourselves. If we stop resisting it and surrender to its wisdom, it can melt our hearts wide open. Like the rainbow at the end of a downpour, sadness reconnects us with tremendous joy. Try the following practices and see where your sadness might bring you.

Practice Tools:

1. Every day we touch sadness through big and small disappointments, hurts, unmet expectations, and conflict. Take twenty minutes to journal about a major sadness in your life, one you can't seem to

shake. Write in "stream of consciousness," which means writing without thinking about it or planning it out or worrying about it making sense. Just sit, uninterrupted, and write down whatever comes.

2. Make friends with sadness. Next time it appears, take time to close your eyes and notice your reactions. See what triggers it and where you feel it in your body. Describe the sensations of it underneath the label. Notice any fear or resistance to feeling sad and which stories it triggers. Allow it to just be present. Getting to know sadness allows you to let it flow through you like changing weather.

3. One morning, when you are feeling extra brave, set aside some time to be with yourself uninterrupted. Lie down on a soft blanket, couch, or bed. Close your eyes. Take some deep breaths in your belly. Say out loud to yourself, "I'm willing to feel whatever sadness I've been unwilling to feel." (This is a powerful intention, so don't do it until you feel ready inside to cry and welcome old griefs buried deep inside.) Say the intention, then continue to take deep breaths, and wait patiently for any sadness to bubble up. Keep breathing and waiting, even if your mind tries to convince you nothing is happening. Sometimes it takes time for our Inner Selves to trust us with these deeper feelings. When sadness arises, breathe directly into it. Really feel how sad you are. It doesn't matter *why* the sadness is there; it only matters that you honor it in a kind, loving way.

4. If you still grieve the loss of someone close to you, write that person a letter. Start, "Dear _____" and write everything that comes to you, in present tense, as if your loved one were still here. Don't censor anything. This might be a beloved parent, spouse, lover, child, or pet you miss sorely. Tell your loved one how much he or she is loved and missed by you. Dare to include *all* your feelings: your anger, rage, grief, fears, resentments, regrets, and unfulfilled dreams. Revisit all the joyful moments.

Making Friends with . . .

Anger

If we are full of rage we have to get
it out of our body. We have to
express it—to ourselves—or it will take
another form, perhaps illness.
—MARION WOODMAN

As a body-centered therapist, I've never met a parent whose out-of-control anger toward their child didn't terrify them. I've never met a client who hasn't felt so enraged at their spouse or lover at times that they were afraid of what they might do—and did and said things they later regretted. I've worked with countless abuse victims who still tremble inside at the mere thought of "making waves" thirty years after their raging parent stopped yelling, or died. The scars and destruction from anger's havoc are around us every day in our homes, in our relationships, and on the evening news.

Like sex, anger is hot, wild, volatile. It makes us feel out of control, and we don't like that. Nor do we know what to do with it. We've had few good role models for anger.

Anger gets a bad rap. In our culture, angry people destroy things and people with their words and fists, even kill in violent rages. Road rage causes accidents and deaths. Misguided, left to our base instincts, anger can get us in a lot of trouble. But anger per se is not the culprit. Violence is. We need to learn how to express anger in healthy ways.

Hundreds of times in therapy, I've witnessed the healthy side of anger. An angry phrase, placed perfectly in a difficult couple's session, is like a strong north wind. It clears the air, cuts through years of dysfunction like a silver sword, and saves the marriage. One woman's husband kept drinking for twenty years, until she got angry enough to place all his belongings on the front porch. That night, he attended his first AA meeting and hasn't had a drink since. Another woman suffered chronic low back pain and bronchitis until she got angry enough to confront her cheating husband. Once she expressed the anger she had been sitting on, her back quit hurting, her energy returned, and she demanded more respect. A kind, soft-spoken, patient man finally exploded in anger toward his wife for being so self-absorbed. Underneath the anger, tears erupted, and he was able to speak the tender, hurt feelings he had withheld for years.

In the deepest throes of indecision regarding whether to stay in her marriage or not, a smart, professional woman who had recently turned forty asked me, "Is love conditional or unconditional?" I paused to feel the deepest truth in my heart of hearts. "Both," I answered. "You need to accept your partner unconditionally, exactly as he or she is, *and* your partner hired you to polish them into a diamond, which only happens by addressing the rough edges and honestly speaking your truth."

Expressing Raw Anger in Healthy Ways

The key is to distinguish between "raw anger" and "processed anger." Raw, instinctual anger comes the instant we feel angry. It flares up from our bellies like a wildfire. It's the hot-lava, four-letter-word anger that wants to lash out at whoever hurt us. Most of us have learned over the years not to unleash this raw anger, but we don't know what to do except stifle it. Usually, it leaks out sideways at the wrong person, burns an ulcer in our stomach, or turns inward, changing into depression. None of these is healthy.

Raw anger needs to be expressed so it doesn't fester in our bodies, but it's best released when we are alone. We can yell loudly in the privacy of our own car, or at home if we feel it is safe to do so, someplace where nobody will hear us or be on the receiving end. After fully releasing our raw anger, we gain clarity to speak our truth to loved ones and friends.

For example, Gloria and Frank came to see me for marital counseling. But their marriage wasn't the real problem. Her job was. And she had grown accustomed to dumping her anger from work on her husband every evening. Not a good formula for a healthy relationship. In our first session, it became clear that she was reliving her abusive childhood in her work setting. She was the only female administrator in a corporation where her passive boss used her as a scapegoat for his inability to make decisions. I suggested that she seriously consider leaving if she wanted to save her health and her marriage.

Before she left our session, I gave her an assignment. Every morning on her hour-long commute to work, and every night on her drive home, I invited her to yell in her car for as long as she felt upset about whatever made her angry that day. (Cars are a great place to do this because other drivers are too absorbed in their own world to notice!)

The next week, she arrived grinning and shaking her head. "I never lasted more than twenty minutes," she chuckled, "but I let it rip. I yelled at everything and everyone who made me angry. I yelled at my spineless boss for blaming me for his mistakes. I yelled at this sick company that blocks me from firing incompetent employees. And I yelled at Howard, who purports to be my friend, but the whole time has been scheming to get my job. By the time I got home, I was yelled out."

"Yes," her husband Frank chimed in. "We actually had some pleasant evenings this week."

Gloria later explored the feelings underneath that fueled her anger. She discovered deep grief she had felt as a young girl when her father discounted her as second class, just someone to marry and bear children. A few months later, when it suited her own personal timing, she resigned. She's enjoying her life for the first time in several years.

Healthy Anger Helps Us Regain Self-Respect

In countless individual sessions, I have watched clients reconnect with their self-respect by hitting a large, stuffed pillow with a tennis racket and claiming their needs in the loudest voice they could muster. (For those who silenced their needs and feelings for years, this was barely above a whisper.) Others never realized how they were allowing their mates or boss to walk all over them until they laid down on my padded futon, kicked one leg and then the other alternately, and kept filling in the phrase, "I feel _____." Until we give our bodies full permission to rage about never feeling heard or seen for who we truly are, as Beings, we cannot access the deep grief and self-worth underneath.

Women, groomed to please and take care of others, finally step into their power for the first time at thirty or forty or fifty years of age, simply by hitting a pillow and yelling, "I deserve to feel heard. I deserve to get my needs met." Men face their lifelong fear of smothering women (derived from their mothers) by hitting pillows and voicing their pain. One man's stomach tension cleared up after he released his pent-up rage about being abused. A woman's chronic back pain went away after she hit a large, stuffed pillow and growled her rage. During a major transition in my life, anger gave me the courage to leave a steady paycheck and start a private practice.

Changing Family Patterns Is Responding Differently

You don't have to rage the way Mom or Dad or your siblings did. You can experiment and carve out new pathways for expressing your anger in healthy ways. So the questions to sit with and wonder about are: "How can I release raw anger in a way that fits me? And how can I speak my processed anger in a way that I will feel heard?"

It's challenging to change old habits, especially ones solidly ingrained for generations. It can even feel hard just to remember to deep breathe, or witness our anger, or respond differently when the fire of anger burns through our minds and bodies. But expanding our awareness enough to *witness* ourselves getting angry is a huge step toward waking up and making new choices. Unconscious choices repeat old habits. Conscious choices open the door for responding with loving compassion, patience, and kindness.

Taking Responsibility Helps Communicate Anger Clearly

We like to believe that so-and-so made us angry. But really, we do it to ourselves. We do it by buying into anger and letting it take us for a ride. We do it by unconsciously allowing the anger to fill our awareness until we can't see straight. We do it by insisting on being right, and making others wrong. We do it by skipping right over our hurt feelings and diving into anger because that makes us feel less vulnerable.

Taking full responsibility for our own reaction frees us to respond differently.

We can't control when anger arises, or how intense it becomes. But we can make friends with it by being curious about it when it arises, noticing how it feels in our bodies and sounds in our minds, and by taking responsibility for expressing it in healthy ways.

The really juicy question to ask, after we have processed our raw anger, is: "Where am I hooked? What is it about this circumstance that triggers such anger in me?" Setting an intention such as, "I'm willing to notice how anger hooks *me*," invites this wisdom into our awareness. Once we have explored our hook—with bosses, parent figures, and good people who are poor listeners—we are less likely to get hooked as badly next time.

Teresa discovered tremendous freedom by exploring her propensity for anger. "For the first time in my life," she told me, "I realized last week, after therapy, that I have a *choice* how I react when my husband and I disagree. For twenty years, I pounced on Fred like a cougar whenever he broke an agreement, whenever he left the bathroom sink dirty, whenever he disappointed me. But this week, when anger came up, I asked myself, 'Where am I hooked?' I told him I needed a time-out and left the living room for fifteen minutes. I closed my eyes and asked,

"What feeling lives underneath my anger?" It was amazing! After twenty years together, I'm terrified of him dying! When I told Fred my real feelings, he didn't run away like he usually does. He stayed and listened. We held each other on the couch for a long time after, without saying anything."

What if we all met anger with curiosity and compassion? What if we all took two or five minutes to exaggerate our raw anger in a safe, private setting? What if we shifted into our Being Self and witnessed our anger, acknowledging gently how challenging it can be at times to be a human being in this fast-paced world? What if we welcomed the hurt, vulnerable feelings fueling our anger and created a safe space to share these with loved ones? How different our relationship with anger, and joy, might be. We would free up tremendous energy and time to ask our Inner Selves, "What does my soul need now?"

Practice Tools:

1. The next time anger strikes, welcome it. Get to know it. Take some deep breaths. Treat its appearance as an opportunity to learn more about yourself, your knee-jerk reaction to anger, and your family patterns. Do you bury it deep inside and hope nobody notices? Do you explode and say things you later regret? Do you feel confused, not knowing what to do? Practice being a curious bystander who *witnesses* anger erupt inside you. Notice from your Being Self what triggers it, how anger feels in your body, and what stories it triggers in your mind.

2. Experiment with finding a comfortable way to express your raw anger. Try yelling in your car on your way home from work. Experiment in the privacy of your own home, alone, with hitting a large stuffed pillow and letting yourself yell your anger. Push your face into a large pillow and growl (the pillow muffles the sound so you can yell without being afraid of others hearing you). Or try stomping your feet into the floor and letting the four-letter words fly. Don't censor yourself. In a safe setting, give your body permission to fully unleash your raw anger. Once your body has permission, it knows exactly how to let it rip. It's a healthy way to move raw anger out of your body and not hurt anyone with it.

3. After you have expressed the raw energy, bring in your curiosity. Sit quietly, close your eyes for a few moments, and ask yourself, "What feeling lives underneath this anger?" Locate where the anger lives in your body and imagine peeking underneath it, as if you were

peeking under a rock. See what feeling is fueling the anger: Hurt? Sadness? Fear? A sense of betrayal or abandonment? Just ask inside, take deep breaths, and listen patiently for your heart to respond.

4. Processed anger is the juicy stuff to share with your mate, older children, friends, or associates. Of course, feeling hurt, sad, or rejected makes you feel much more vulnerable than unleashing anger on somebody. So create a safe setting for yourself and them. Find a time that is convenient for both of you. Ask the other person if he or she is willing to not interrupt you until you say you are finished. (This way, if that person does jump in defending him- or herself, all you need to say is, "Please, don't interrupt me, as you agreed.") *Share your whole truth*, which includes any fears you might be feeling about sharing, or how it feels inside you to share in this new, vulnerable way. Instead of saying, "You made me angry," take full responsibility for your anger and teach the other person about yourself. It might sound like, "I notice when you did or said _____, I felt extremely angry. When I explored my strong reaction inside, I realized I felt betrayed by your lack of support. How you could most support me right now is _____." By teaching the other person what you feel and what you need, you create more closeness rather than pushing him or her away, which is what unconsciously expressed anger always does.

Making Friends with . . .

Resentment

The greatest obstacle to connecting
with our joy is resentment.
—PEMA CHODRON

Resentment is slippery. It hides in our unconscious like a snake, convincing us to withhold love and withdraw emotionally because we are right, and the other person is so wrong. But all it really does is spit at the thought of forgiveness and force us to live in the past, powerless to create positive change.

We live in the Age of Resentment. Many of us spend years resenting our parents for not giving us the unconditional love we deserved, even though they never had it to give. Many of us spent the eighties and nineties resenting them for dumping generations of alcoholism, abuse, perfectionism, and self-loathing on us to clean up. We resented our fathers for being absent, or overbearing, or inappropriately sexual, or spineless. We resented our mothers for controlling us, neglecting us, or smothering and guilt-tripping us. But feeling resentful doesn't dissolve all the unconscious fear and shame from our ancestors that we still carry in our bodies like family heirlooms.

Resentments are often completely legitimate. We have every right to feel resentful. Fathers, mothers, stepfathers, uncles, aunts, and grandparents who abused or molested us deserve to face charges. Parents who used their innocent children to meet their own emotional needs deserve to hear about the damage they caused. Husbands, wives, and parents need to hear what it feels like to be overpowered, manipulated, and shamed.

But at what point does holding onto old resentments cause us more harm than good? When do we let it go and forgive? And what price do we pay, in our health and our love relationships, for holding onto them? It's impossible to be fully present in a love relationship *and* hold onto hurt and resentment. It's impossible to stand fully in joy *and* secretly cling to old resentments. Resentment steals joy like nothing else. It cheats us out of wholesome loving contact with those we love. It destroys perfectly good relationships.

Making the Wall of Resentment Conscious

Show me a couple who has been together two years, and I'll show you their baby wall of resentment just starting to be built. Show me a couple who has been together ten or twenty years, and their unspoken wall of resentment is so high they can't see each other anymore. Yet we tend not to speak in terms of "resentments." If we talk at all, we talk about hurts, disappointments, mistrust, and broken agreements. Often, resentments are buried so deep in our bellies, so far below our awareness, that we only speak in terms of, "he never . . ." and, "she never . . ." or, "he always . . ." and, "she always . . ." Our bodies act out our resentments by being too busy to connect, too tired to make love.

Sometimes we say, "I forgive you." But we can't truly forgive until we first identify out loud all the little and not-so-little resentments we are holding onto, followed by what we need. The truth is, if we love somebody, if we live with somebody and raise children with them, they are going to hurt and disappoint us along the way. And we will hurt and disappoint them. It's impossible to avoid. We are so busy reenacting our own version of our parents' unconscious habits, or feeding our belief that "nobody cares about my needs," that we hurt others without realizing it. And they are too busy reinforcing their unconscious beliefs to address it. It takes tremendous inner strength and maturity to see ourselves, and someone we love, clearly.

The piece that the minister, rabbi, or priest often leaves out is that we don't have much clue who we have fallen in love with until *after* the first two years of a relationship. It takes two years to really know someone, and to finally feel safe enough ourselves to drag out our family heirlooms—the unconscious baggage buried inside that needs to be loved. Our moody sulking, jealous outbursts, and self-righteous judgments are really asking, "Will you still love me, even if I do *this*!!!" It's in intimate relationship where the parts of ourselves that feel unlovable (those places inside we had to reject earlier) bubble up to the surface to be loved. Until we become skillful at talking about these tender places, we act out the ugliest parts in front of loved ones. Resentment is no exception. Left unspoken, festering inside, it's the kind of thing that, over time, leads to affairs, illness, or depression.

Julie was referred to me for depression. She had suffered severe fatigue for five years. Her doctor ran every medical test in the book on her, but they revealed no physical reason for her tiredness. She dragged through each day, even after eight or nine hours of sleep, and napped during her lunch hour. But extra sleep didn't alleviate her fatigue.

As she told me stories about her husband, her grown children, her work, and her friends, I detected a common thread in each relationship: resentment. By her late forties, resentment had painted her entire life into a tight, boring corner. She had written off her husband years ago as incapable of carrying on an intellectual conversation. She still resented her son for getting arrested at sixteen for drugs (even though now, ten years later, her son was a single parent working full-time). She resented her daughter for marrying the wrong man. She resented her boss because, five years earlier, in a staff meeting, her boss had embarrassed her in front of her colleagues. She even stopped speaking to her best friend because her friend had done something that offended her principles. She learned this pattern from her parents.

Julie prided herself on being a woman of principles. However, nobody could live up to her principles, not even herself. This narrow window of "acceptable behavior" found her, and those close to her, guilty of being human. It drained the life force out of her.

Forgiveness is the shortcut to dissolving resentments. But forgiveness didn't come easy for Julie. Her pride blocked her from discussing her feelings out loud, even with her husband of thirty-some years. She tried "thinking forgiveness" in her head, but that didn't work. Eventually, she promised to break the ice by talking to her son. "I ignored him the past few years when he dropped by to visit," she explained, "so I apologized to him. I told him I was trying this forgiveness thing. He laughed. Now we're buddies again."

The next week, she invited the friend she hadn't spoken to for years over for a barbecue. "We talked for hours," she said. "I remembered how she had always felt like the sister I never had. I figured it had been too long to bring up what happened some years ago, but when I finally found the courage to tell her, she apologized. Tears filled her eyes, and she said how much she'd missed me."

Over the next month, Julie responded differently to her husband. She initiated conversations with him at the dinner table, asked him questions, and found him surprisingly capable of good conversation. "Even though I've lived with him all these years," she said with a twinkle in her eyes, "I don't really know him. But it's fun getting to know him all over again."

Julie had to step past her pride to notice all her judgments. She practiced "tagging" her judgments without buying into them. Whenever she thought of it, she practiced replacing judgments with, "I choose joy." When her boss offered her a huge promotion last fall, Julie turned it down. "I don't know how many years I have left," she said, "but I know now I want to spend them enjoying my husband, my children, and my grandchildren."

Resentment Strangles Our Love Feelings, If We Let It

Resentment howls through our lives like a bitter, cold wind, if we don't address it. It's not hot, like anger. It doesn't propel us to explode with our truth, like anger. Instead it slowly, methodically, invisibly strangles our love feelings. It shuts down our joy, sometimes for years. It convinces us to withdraw into our busy, predictable lives. It schemes up stories about why we can't trust the person closest to us anymore. It wins whenever we don't own our resentment and instead project it onto others. Inside, we sneer, "He never listens. She doesn't care." Outside, we lie and say, "I'm fine. I'm just feeling quiet (for years)." Bottom line, it steals our aliveness without us even realizing it.

My own mother could have taught a graduate course in resentment. She was married to my father for twenty-six years. She resented him twenty-four of those years. She once told me, years after I'd left home, that the first two years of her marriage were "pretty good." That would have been before they had children, when they lived in a small apartment in Fargo, North Dakota and rode bikes everywhere because they couldn't afford a car. Over the years, every hurt, every disappointment, every broken agreement was tossed on her resentment pile until she couldn't stand to look at him. She finally divorced him thirty-three years ago. But she never forgave him. Even on her deathbed, she refused to call my eighty-five-year-old father and say, "I forgive you."

My mother taught me well. But I'm sure she never dreamed I would turn it against her and resent her for being depressed and suicidal when I was a child. I did, for two decades. I resented her for not being more available as a mother when I was growing up. I resented her for using my brother and me as the excuse for staying with my father, the man she swore she didn't love. I resented her for popping uppers and downers just to make it through the day. But I never realized the high price I paid for such resentment until my forties, when chronic digestive irritation plagued me for six long years. No doctor, acupuncturist, naturopath, or medication was able to heal this irritation. Only acknowledging all the resentment I carried in my bowels did. Only forgiving her did.

Responding with Compassion to Resentment

It's vital to stop buying into our resentment. Notice it whenever it pays a visit. Get to know how it sounds in your head, and how it feels in your belly. Resentment is not right under the surface like sadness or anger. We routinely say, "I feel sad. I'm hurt. I feel angry." But we rarely admit to feeling resentful. That's because we rarely realize we are resentful. The first step to responding differently is saying yes to whatever we feel resentful about without judging ourselves for it. Writing your resentments down on a piece of paper is a great way to acknowledge them to yourself. The second step is witnessing your behavior and actions. If you notice yourself cuddling less, losing interest in sexual and nonsexual touch, staying busy, creating extra work for yourself, you might ask yourself, "What resentment am I holding against my mate?" If you find yourself sick on Monday morning, dreading work, or feeling extra tired at work, ask yourself, "What resentment am I holding against my boss? What lie do I need to look at regarding work?" Making your resentments conscious is mandatory in order to let them go.

Responding differently requires you to witness the feeling of resentment as one small part of who you really are, on the Being level. Be curious. Notice what triggers it. Say to yourself, "Hmmmm, I'm feeling resentful. I wonder what that's about. I wonder what payoff I'm getting from feeling resentful: Do I get to hide my more vulnerable feelings? Do I get to build a case against trusting this person? Do I get to play victim?" Notice and *talk about* your resentment with someone close to you. "I notice I still feel resentful about you flirting with my best friend last year. I experience it as a tightness in my diaphragm. It's triggering thoughts such as, 'I can't trust you with my real feelings' or, 'there's never any room for my needs.'" Use it as a tool to teach others about yourself.

Resentment, unrecognized, unacknowledged, comes with too high of a price tag. We have to get beyond all our good, legitimate reasons for feeling resentful, and open our hearts. We have to open our eyes wide to see whatever heavy resentment we carry in our bodies and let it go. We need to stretch our hearts wide to see all the ways we, too, have unconsciously hurt, betrayed, disappointed, and abandoned others. We need to be willing to forgive and forgive and forgive. We have to step fully into this moment fresh and unencumbered. We need to say yes to all the resentments we carry inside, witness them, and respond to each one with an open, compassionate heart.

Practice Tools:

1. Take a half hour to sit down with a piece of paper and list anything you feel resentful about. List any and all resentments you hold against your parents (alive or deceased). List any resentments toward past and current lovers, your spouse, your ex, your children, and your friends. Don't hold back. The best way to make resentments conscious is to totally indulge them. Say yes to each one of them.

2. Discover what you are getting out of holding onto your resentment. Finish this statement over and over again, writing down the first thing that comes to your mind: "As long as I feel resentful, I don't have to _____ (risk sharing vulnerable feelings, step out of playing victim and take responsibility, etc.)" Another way of getting underneath the old habit is to keep completing the sentence, "As long as I keep my resentment to myself, I get to avoid _____."

3. Respond to your resentment from a place of curiosity. Notice it without buying into it or letting yourself run away into some project. Set an intention to notice and *talk about* your resentments with loved ones from this "curious" perspective. Love yourself for feeling resentful, even if you held onto it for years, then let it go. Hold your resentment in loving compassion and joy.

Making Friends with . . .

Fear

*When you finally, completely face
fear itself, it is nowhere to be found.
Fear can never survive total
meeting with consciousness.*

—GANGAJI

A h, fear. Our egos like to make fear a nonissue, telling us that we moved past all that years ago. But our own refusal to be completely honest with ourselves allows fear to run our lives, unconsciously. Until we truly open our eyes and hearts, and get to know fear at this deep level, we continue to buy into it and obey it like some high priest or parent figure. After all, inside our heads, fear sounds so rational, so logical, so reasonable. Of course, some fear is good, and necessary. When fear warns us not to put our hand on a hot burner, or drive too fast near a cliff, it's a good friend. The Dalai Lama calls this instinctual response to a danger signal, "wholesome fear." As we get to know the nature of fear, we more easily destinguish between "wholesome fear" and the "fear of illusion."

As small children, when life looked so overwhelming to us at times, we had to bow to fear, as our conditioning taught us, to ensure our survival. Now, as conscious adults, our job is to see fear as fear, say yes to it, and witness it without succumbing to it.

As an experiment, designate one week for noticing fear thoughts. Say to yourself, "I'm willing to recognize any fears that enter my awareness this week." With a nonjudgmental curiosity, see what triggers fear, how long it lasts, and what feelings follow it. You will soon realize how much you can't control fear. None of us can. Fear thoughts come and go, moving through us as they please. The one thing we can control, however, is how we respond. If we say yes to fear, we can be momentarily amused by fear's great imagination, then move on to creating what we most want. It's always our choice.

Labeling Fear and Letting It Go

The best way to let go of fear, paradoxically, is to pay very close attention when it lands on our doorstep. Be open and curious. Learn the "language of fear." Don't block insights by letting your ego say that you have already moved past fear. Start the morning with an intention: "I'm willing to recognize fear today in its many disguises, including when it sounds very logical and reasonable." Practice labeling it, "fearing, fearing" when it arises, then let it go. Refocus in the present moment on what your hands are doing, what your eyes are seeing, what your ears are hearing, or how the air is flowing in and out of your body.

Fear loves to scare us most about past and future circumstances (things that already happened and that we can't change *or* things that might possibly happen at some future date). It usually arrives couched in "what if…" statements, which is a dead giveaway. "*What if* I don't save enough for retirement and end up homeless? *What if* he or she doesn't really love me and I am rejected? *What if* I follow my dream and can't make a decent living at it? *What if* I finally say how bored I feel in this relationship, and it explodes into a huge fight? *What if* I go through surgery and chemo and die anyway?" The truth is, *nobody knows what the next moment will bring—and neither does fear.*

If fear is doing its job right, it wedges doubt between ourselves and our wildest dreams. It judges us, scares us, criticizes us—whatever it has to do to "keep us safe." (A never-ending task in fear's eyes.) It gets us to treat fear as an amendment to the Ten Commandments: "Thou shalt obey fear at all costs." It sees itself as keeping us from ever getting hurt, rejected, abandoned, or brokenhearted again, and it takes this job very seriously. Its intentions are honorable. But its means are quite archaic. When it holds us hostage for hours (or years), painting bleak images of disasters in our minds, it robs us of our joy. If we are not careful, it can talk us into ruining perfectly good relationships.

We can't control which fears come when. We may be having fabulous sex when, suddenly, fear whispers in our ear, "What if you get pregnant?" Or if you have been trying to get pregnant for a while, it whispers, "What if you don't get pregnant, *again*?" We might have a slow week at work, and suddenly fear joins in, filling our minds with catastrophic images of losing money, closing our doors, and having to file for bankruptcy—all within two minutes! Give it credit for its great imagination. Then switch channels.

Fear is an all-occasion standby. We can count on it showing up, planting a seed of doubt, just when we are happy and feeling on top of the world. It comes when we are down in the dumps, already feeling like a failure. It comes anytime, any place. It especially comes when we are about to take a risk, start a new business, or dive into a new relationship. The trick is to expect it. Welcome it. Witness the grand, elaborate story it's manifesting at breakneck speed. Then label it and let it go.

Fear tests us. It sees how long it can hold our attention before we finally yell, "Busted!" If it had its way, fear would keep us tucked away in a closet down in the basement inside our fireproof home inside a locked gate our whole lives. That's why it is important, after recognizing and labeling it, to respond from your mature Being Self.

Respond to Fear with Reassurance and Acceptance

In order to transform our lives, to become all of who we can be, we need to greet fear with love when it arrives. Meditation teacher Jack Kornfield once said in a dharma talk, "What people most want is to be heard, to be listened to, to feel acknowledged . . ." That is what feelings want, too, even fear. Fear is our childlike Inner Self crying out, "This change scares me. It's not familiar. I'm afraid. Can you please talk to me, reassure me, tell me that I'm still safe, even now?" It is like a six-year-old coming to us in the middle of the night terrified of a nightmare. The last thing the child needs is for us to buy into the nightmare and get scared, too. Like the child, our Inner Self needs reassurance.

Fear resides deep inside our bodies. When we have an angry outburst, touch deep sadness, or bask in resentment, we can always find fear underneath, fueling these feelings. Fear hides deep in our unconscious. It is so primal and basic. We fear losing what we have. We fear not getting what we want. And we fear getting what we don't want and desperately try to avoid. The motivating factor for most unconscious actions in our lives boils down to fear.

That's why it's so critical to recognize fear when fear is speaking to us. As we nurture our relationship with our mature Being Self who easily recognizes and lets go of fear, we come to hold even fear in loving acceptance and compassion. As we do so, inner joy begins to naturally radiate through our whole being like sunlight. The more we loosen our tight grip on fear, the more we hear the soft quiet inner voice of love, encouraging us to trust our feelings, trust our hearts, and speak our truth.

Every moment, we make choices. Sometimes, we consciously choose to love our fear. Of course, when we state it so directly, it sounds so illogical to our mind. It sounds even crazier to reassure that childlike part of ourselves inside with loving words of comfort when it touches fear. But as we practice this, and as we have a bodily experience of loving even our fears, our hearts feel much lighter, freer, more spacious and joyful. Responding to fear with loving acceptance brings us one step closer to who we truly are.

Practice Tools:

1. Pick a fear that is up in your life. It may be fear of not getting what you want, fear of failure or intimacy, or fear of losing control. Take five minutes to exaggerate it. Pretend you're in drama class and your role is to act out this fear. Find the "posture" of it. (For example, "fear of rejection" is rounded shoulders, tucked pelvis, with the head down.) Say out loud what this fear tells you in your head. (It may sound like, "I never get what I want," "That's a stupid idea," or, "I'm nuts to give up my steady paycheck.") Saying our fears out loud usually makes us crack up. They sound much funnier, and less reasonable, than they do in our minds. In a pinch, say, "I am willing to feel joy, even now."

2. Set aside time to get to know fear. Set an intention each morning: "I'm willing to see fear in any ways I've been unwilling to see it." Notice how it talks to you. Whether meditating, commuting to work, shopping, or sitting at your computer, whenever you notice a fear, ask inside: "What triggered it? How do I react? (Do I deny it? Resist it? Pretend it doesn't exist? Indulge it?) How long does it stay? Which stories does it play? What happens when I label it, 'fearing, fearing'?"

3. As you grow more comfortable with leaning into fear, try finishing this sentence: "When I feel afraid, I become _____ (anxious? depressed? numb? lonely?). Just ask, take deep breaths, and listen for answers to bubble up from inside. Often our favorite addictions mask our fear and prevent us from facing it.

4. Pick one thing you are especially afraid of. Notice what stories it generates. Every time you notice it, witness it and let your Being Self reassure your Inner Self. Be the mature Being holding fear in loving compassion. Genuinely ask your heart, "What place inside me is asking for acceptance here?" Wait patiently for the answer. Try saying, "I love myself for feeling afraid, and I love myself for needing to reject this part of myself." (It might be fear of not being loved, or fear of not being really seen and heard for who you are.) Whatever it is, love the fear.

5. Accept total responsibility for your fear. Wonder, "What is my payoff for buying into this fear?" (Buying into fears allows us to not try, not risk, and not speak our truth.) Take this one step further and

ask inside yourself: "If I wasn't afraid, what small or big changes might I make in my work? In my health? In my love relationship? In my sex life? In my social life? In how I spend my free time? In how I respond to my heart's longings?" Remember to always turn complaints into requests, with yourself and your relationships. Be patient with the process.

Depression and Hopelessness

We must inquire what . . . is asking
for acceptance and compassion,
and ask ourselves, "Can I touch with love
whatever I have closed my heart to?"

—JACK KORNFIELD

A dear friend called last night. After chatting a few minutes, she told me about her current health crises. "My insomnia and digestive problems are worse than they've been in two years," she said, "so all my extra money coming in from work now is going to healers. But on the deep Being level," she added, "I know I'm okay. I know I'm being asked by spirit to hold my symptoms, and my despair, in compassion and love."

My friend has been cultivating deep compassion and lovingkindness toward herself and others for the past thirty years. We, too, can learn to hold our despairing, hopeless, depressed feelings in loving compassion. All we need is the courage to stop resisting these dark feelings, some quiet alone time to get to know these feelings better, and a willingness to respond differently. I would even go so far as to say that feeling depressed can be a good teacher.*

First, like my friend, we need to be willing to say yes to what is true. That takes guts. We need to acknowledge that, indeed, it has landed on our doorstep. We need to stop denying it. Stop skirting around it. Stop trying to avoid being labeled "depressed."

When it strikes, we usually go to great lengths to prove to ourselves, and others, that we are not depressed. Meanwhile, we are chanting under our breath, "I am not depressed, I am not depressed; I'm just having a bad day" all the way to work and all the way home. We frantically practice positive thinking, while watching ourselves sink deeper and deeper into quicksand. Or we read *Oprah* magazine to learn the latest quick fix. Or we see an ad for Zoloft on TV, consider it synchro-

---

* It's important to distinguish between clinical depression and "feeling depressed." Clinical depression is more serious and requires working with a good physician you can trust to find the right medication for you.

nistic, and call our doctor the next morning, only to join the millions of adults and children on antidepressants.

I know. I was terrified of catching it for twenty years, literally. I was so scared that I might be prone to depression (and suicidal thoughts, like my mother) that I took up running. First I ran three miles a day at the Berkeley High track, then six and nine miles around the neighborhood. Soon I was racing in marathons and half-marathons.

For years, I told friends, and myself, that I was "training" for the next 10K race or marathon, but really I desperately needed my endorphin high everyday. And God bless the friend or lover who tried to interfere with this. Some days after my daily run, I would mountain bike, African dance, or hike—any movement to keep the endorphins flowing. It was great for my heart and spirit, better than the alcohol and Valium my mother used, but still I was running away from some mythical depression I had never actually felt.

Luckily, in my early forties, low-back pain stopped this compulsive behavior. As I lay flat on my back on my living room sofa, I began crying "for no apparent reason." And couldn't stop. All the grief and fear I had no room to express as a small child, terrified that my mother really would kill herself one dark night, came flooding out. I had finally given my Inner Self the time, space, and permission to feel everything I had been afraid to feel. When I finished grieving, this radiant joy filled my whole being. I'll never forget it. It was pure joy, not dependent on a good run, or great sex, or anything. It seems so silly now, to spend years running away from a feeling that just wants to be expressed. I still run occasionally, though I prefer hiking. But I'm no longer running away.

Dropping Down underneath the Big, Scary Label

The word "depressed" comes with such heavy baggage, especially these days. The mere mention of the word triggers overwhelming fears inside. We wonder, "If I'm depressed, will I stay depressed for the rest of my life, like Mom, or Dad, or Uncle Harry? Will I have to take antidepressants the rest of my life? And if I surrender to these feelings, will I be able to function, to keep working and care for my kids? Or will I lose my job, my relationship, everything, and just lie in bed all day, not caring anymore?"

Rather than be overwhelmed by the label, let's explore the territory underneath. Next time you feel down, lean into it. Bring your curiosity to it, as if you were watching the Discovery channel. Close your eyes, take some deep breaths, and *locate where* you feel hopeless in your body. Where does it live, inside? Does it appear as a heaviness in your chest? Or do you experience it more as a pressure or tightness in your diaphragm or belly? Acknowledge any fear you might feel about tuning into it. Rather than imposing any ideas about it from your head, just listen to your body. Notice whatever is true for you in this moment. Try to notice it without labeling your feeling as good or bad.

In southwest Colorado, where I live, I have a good reputation for working with depression. Doctors refer their depressed patients to me, probably because I'm not afraid of it. I see it as a big red flag, signaling an important crossroad in someone's life. Unlike a fleeting sadness or anger, feeling depressed demands our attention.

Feeling Depressed Is Our Inner Self Asking Us to Listen

The image of "depression" in my mind looks like this: Our wise Being Self (who loves us more than we can imagine) is standing at the top of the bleachers waving a huge, red banner, shouting at the top of its lungs: "Stop! Stop what you're doing! Slow down! You're heading in the wrong direction! You're painting yourself into a corner, a corner you're going to hate. You'll fall off a cliff if you keep going. You need to listen to your heart now, to your feelings and longings. You need to change an old belief you're still carrying around that's not working anymore. It's time to voice those needs and feelings that are stuck in your throat. **Pay Attention!!!**"

In other words, the huge "tilt" buzzer is going off inside, warning us we are out of balance. It's our own, personal, inner red flag. Usually we've had some subtler warning signs before the big "D" arrives. We may have been feeling sad "for no apparent reason." Or we notice ourselves getting sick more often than usual. Maybe that chronic pain won't resolve itself, no matter how many healers we see. Maybe we've withdrawn from life, feeling like we are just going through the motions. It's always easier to look back, in hindsight, and recognize the warning signs.

Unfortunately, we are taught in Western culture to override our body signals, numb our pain with medication, and discount our feelings. I tell clients that I would be out of a job if we were taught how to listen to our bodies and feelings, and practiced speaking our truth. Our Being Self does eventually get our attention though. When it needs to, when we ignore those signals long enough, it calls in the "big guns": chronic pain, work-stopping illness, life-threatening disease, and feeling depressed.

It demanded Jim's attention. Jim, already on antidepressants, was referred to me by his doctor. For twenty years, since his first bout of depression in college, he had dealt with it himself. He threw himself into bike racing, training hard every night after work. He mastered positive thinking. He "beat" depression by staying preoccupied with starting a new business every two years. But by his mid-forties, his tricks stopped working.

Jim scared himself. He found himself thinking suicide was preferable to living. At first, this thought only happened once or twice a month, when he was really upset. Then it came more and more frequently. When it appeared daily, he ran to his doctor.

Jim had lived his life, and held depression at bay, by following logic and reason. So I needed to give him some logical reason to lean on. "There is a saying in therapy," I told Jim. "If what you are doing isn't working, try the opposite. Now the way you have been reacting to your depression—pretending it's not there, distracting your mind, trying to talk yourself out of it—isn't working, so would you be willing, as an experiment, to try the opposite?" He furrowed his brow, then slowly nodded.

"OK then," I pounced on my chance. "I want you to stand up and indulge your depression. Exaggerate it. Walk around the room, say the depressed thoughts out loud. How does it convince you that death is preferable to life? Bring it out into the open air."

He scratched his neck, puzzled. "I never was too good at this acting stuff," he protested. "But my doctor highly recommended you, so I guess I could give it a whirl." He stiffly walked around the room, not fully convinced he had come to the right office.

Finally, he spoke. "It berates me for not sticking with that high-paying job in L.A., reminding me that I'd have been a millionaire by now. It says any teenager could do my job—landscaping. And it tells me that my father would be a lot more proud of me if I made more money. Then it says that nobody would really miss me if I die."

"It's so judgmental," I reflected. "Close your eyes a moment. I'm going to say those same words back to you, and I want you to notice how the heavy judgments feel in your body." He listened patiently. Then his jaw began to drop open. "My God," he said. "I feel this unbearable pressure right here, in my upper chest. Come to think of it, I've felt it for a long time." When I had him breathe into that place, he touched deep sadness.

By voicing his depression out loud, and breathing into the heaviness in his chest, Jim began to witness his depression without realizing it. He recognized that who he was, in his core, was much more than his depressed thoughts and feelings. But he wasn't home free yet. The turning point came weeks later, right in the middle of his workday. It came when he took full responsibility for feeling depressed.

"I felt really upset with my coworker for not being able to repair any machinery," he said. "Three tractors were broken. I was tinkering with them, steaming under my collar. And then I got it. I saw clearly that I had fallen into my 'feel depressed' groove in my mind. I knew if I kept upsetting myself, I'd get really down. So I stopped what I was doing. I looked up at that turquoise blue sky that I love and took some deep breaths. I mumbled the depressed thoughts out loud to myself until I broke up laughing. In that moment, with the hot summer sun on my body, and the red-winged blackbirds singing to me in the tall grass, my depression floated away. I wasn't immersed in it anymore."

"Ever since that moment, I don't seem to feel depressed anymore," he grinned. "My mind is in training, the way I trained my body for racing all these years. Whenever I catch myself judging others, or judging myself, or thinking despairing thoughts, I stop what I'm doing and focus on the present. I ask myself, 'What am I hearing? What am I seeing, right now?' From this expanded view, the depression shrinks to manageable size."

Jim found help with antidepressants and by coming to know his depression intimately. However, this doesn't work for everyone. If you think you are experiencing clinical depression, find a good physician or naturopath who can explain the warning signs and help you find proper treatment.

Surrounding Our Dark Feelings with Compassion and Joy

We can all get to know our hopelessness and depressed feelings better. In fact, living in everyday joy requires that. It requires shifting identities into the powerful, creative Being that we are, no matter what feeling has grabbed our attention. It is touching the unlimited joy and love in our core. From that stance, we can easily acknowledge whatever feeling is moving through us in any given moment. All feelings become less scary, more manageable. Remember, our pure inner joy is always there, underneath the feelings, thoughts, and stories consuming our attention. Whenever our joy is covered up, it's our job to *un*cover it. To remember it. To surround feelings with the pure joy that lives deep inside. To pause, stop what we are doing, and bring ourselves into the present by noticing what we are seeing and hearing.

With this loving gesture, we say yes to whatever thoughts or feelings are moving through us and stop buying into them. From this place, we easily recognize that who we are is so much bigger than our feelings, thoughts, and judgments. Since only a part of us is feeling depressed, our Being Self tenderly holds that part in loving compassion. Responding with kindness and compassion is how we reconnect with our pure joy of Being.

Practice Tools:

1. Next time you feel depressed, try moving underneath that big, scary label. Say yes by leaning into it rather than running away from it. Set aside a half hour. Lie down, close your eyes, and take some deep breaths in your belly. Be curious and wonder: "Where do I feel hopeless or depressed in my body? What does it feel like? What thoughts is it triggering in my head? (Just witness your thoughts without judgment, as if you were watching someone else's thoughts, not your own.) What stories is it telling me? What price do I pay for buying into these?" By posing questions to your inner wisdom and patiently listening for words or images to pop into your awareness, you engage your intuition.

2. Often we unconsciously add to our own depressed feelings by worrying about money, our relationship, or work—focusing in the past or future rather than the present. As you grow more comfortable and less scared with feeling depressed, *tune in to the energy underneath the "story."* Try lying down or sitting up, close your eyes, take several deep breaths, and locate where you feel depressed in your body. Engage your willingness by setting an intention. Say to yourself, "I'm willing to feel the *energy* of even this feeling." As you deep breathe, imagine exhaling directly down into the center of that feeling in your body. Hang out with it. Really be with it. Feel how depressed you really feel in this moment. Notice the color and texture of "feeling depressed." Stay with the energy of it for several minutes. (When I do this exercise, my feeling transforms into an energy vibration that spreads throughout my entire body. I become filled with immense joy for no reason my mind can explain.)

3. Usually, some unconscious belief is fueling our depressed feelings. As you identify this old belief, it breaks the habitual pattern. Next

time you feel down or depressed, bring your curiosity. Close your eyes, deep breathe, and notice where you feel depressed in your body. Then focus on your heart and ask, "What belief is fueling my feeling depressed?" Ask, take deep breaths, let go of your thoughts that want to rush in with a quick answer, and listen for whatever bubbles into your awareness. It is often a core belief left over from childhood, such as, "I'm not good enough," "I'm unworthy," or, "I don't deserve to have my needs met." You can change old beliefs on a dime, if you are willing. Just say out loud what you want your new belief to sound like. "I am good enough" or, "I deserve to have my feelings heard and my needs met." Repeat this intention every morning to yourself several times, then watch it take hold in your life. Once you consciously recognize what belief is fueling your depressed feelings, and you fully express your blocked feelings, you are responding with compassion and kindness. This is the pathway to pure joy (and it makes no sense to mind at first, so don't let this stop you from trying).

Making Friends with . . .

Shame

Shame was put upon you. It is not yours.
Your soul need not be limited by shame.
—MARION WOODMAN

Shame is a dirty word. We don't talk about shame, not in our modern civilized Western culture. We don't say, "Hey, my shame is up today." In fact, few of us admit to ourselves that we might carry shame in our bodies, even if it originated from our ancestors. Fewer still even know it's there, it's so well tucked away under the basement of our psyches. Shame evolves from life events that nobody ever talks about, the off-limit topics among family members: the hushed abortion, the pregnant teenager, the cousins who played "doctor" after puberty, the incest that nobody talked about, crazed Aunt Mildred whose manic-depression went undiagnosed, Uncle Harry the lush, or Mom's nervous breakdown. It's not the events themselves, but the silence around these family secrets, that creates shame and passes it on from generation to generation. We could just as well let it lie in the basement, if it didn't damage our self-worth so strongly.

Carrying shame in the deep, dark underbelly of our bellies, our genitals, and our bowels is like carrying poison inside. Over the years, as we go about our lives, it silently festers in our stomachs, intestines, colons, and genitals without ever showing its true colors. It's like a thief, stealing our aliveness, our joy, our life force. It's insidious. It lives deep in the unconscious, where no light shines. It slithers silently around our bellies and intestines like a snake, barely breathing, invisible to the naked eye. It blinds us to our own beautiful Being Self. It silences our voices. Eventually, we don't just stop voicing our needs and feelings—we stop having them altogether.

You may recognize shame's voice more than its face. It's the voice that whispers in your ear, "Hide! Stay invisible! Fit in, at all costs! Don't let anyone see your gifts. Don't stand out. Don't make waves. If you let them see who you really are, they'll see the huge, black, empty hole inside you and prove you're 'not good enough.'" It talks us out of our basic human needs for touch, contact, affection, and sexual pleasure, making us feel deeply ashamed for even asking, or wanting to ask. It stamps our needs and feelings with one bold, black word: "**Undeserving**."

Like drugs, we pretend in this culture that shame doesn't exist. This forces it underground, even deeper into our unconscious. Even with a skilled therapist, it can take months (or years) of working through anger, resentment, grief, and fear before we even start to identify the deep, invisible layers of shame. It requires even more awareness and courage to uncover the ancestral shame buried deep in our bowels, minds, and cells.

Some of us carry shame for growing up poorer than other families, getting a divorce, having an abortion or two, or being in recovery. Others carry shameful scars from their childhoods for the color of their skin, their sexual preference, being too smart or not smart enough, too fat or too skinny, having large breasts or small breasts or small penises, or for living in a physically challenged body. We carry shame for being different, looking different, somehow not fitting in to the narrow, picture-perfect image of "normal." Reasons for feeling ashamed in this judgment-prone culture crop up every day. The hard part is acknowledging to ourselves that we might be carrying shame in our bodies, shame we can't see or feel. That takes courage, openness, and trust.

To our logical minds, it makes no sense to lean into shame or dredge it up. Most of us consider ourselves lucky if we can, somehow, forget about it and focus on fun things. The only problem is, shame clouds our joy. It blocks us from feeling the natural joy and aliveness that is our birthright, and it does this without our even knowing it. If we knew how strongly unconscious shame affects our lives, our health, and our sense of self, we would all race to the front of the line to face it, as if our hair were on fire.

Inviting Invisible Shame into Our Awareness

The quickest way to let shame lead us to joy is to be willing to acknowledge it.

I will never forget Lorraine. In her late forties, Lorraine was a soft-spoken, shy woman of few words who seemed apologetic for even existing. She was referred by a close friend. She never mentioned shame. She had no clue how much it strangled her joy. She spoke of depression, loneliness, and grief. She had lacked meaning in her life since her children had grown up. Her husband had died in an accident, so she raised her children alone. "I have trouble saying no to men's sexual advances," she said, "so I avoid them."

One day, as she witnessed her voice of depression, she remembered something she hadn't thought about in years. She remembered her grandfather molesting her. Even as she spoke the words to me thirty-some years later, she quickly covered her mouth with her hand, as if she would get in big trouble for divulging the family secret. She had never told anyone, not her mother or her father, not her best friend, not even her husband.

"I was ten at the time," she recalled. "Grandpa loved me much more than either of my parents. He spent time with me, bought me candy and dolls . . . I was Grandpa's special little girl. So when he began touching my privates, I knew right away it was wrong, but I couldn't tell on him. I couldn't bear the loneliness if he was prohibited from seeing me. I would be stuck alone with my parents, and I couldn't stand that."

Lorraine wept softly. "I changed after that," she continued. "I became quiet at school. I avoided my friends. I felt odd, different, like I didn't belong. I guess I was ashamed." I had her lie down, close her eyes, and locate where she felt the shame in her body. "It's like a black, empty hole down here, in my pelvis," she said.

As she breathed into the center of that black hole, she touched deep grief. She grieved for that trusting little girl who was silenced by her grandfather's actions. For years, she had felt numb below her neck, disconnected from her feelings and passion, as if her body didn't belong to her. As she breathed deeply, waves of sadness washed over her. Afterwards, she grinned a peaceful grin, as if she was ten years old again. "I feel different, energized, alive," she said. "More alive than I've felt in years." She continued to have trouble speaking up, but she made a strong commitment to voice her needs.

Two years later, she e-mailed me. "In my work with you, I learned to speak my truth. Most of those times, the absolute last thing I wanted to do was stand up and move with my feelings or exaggerate some gesture. A part of me just didn't want to be seen.

"So it was pretty remarkable that, in a recent workshop dealing with gender issues, I asked the facilitators to give me some time on the agenda one morning to speak about my story of sexual abuse. I took the talking stick, stood at the center of that large circle of women and men, and told my story . . . I wanted the men in that circle to understand how early, and how thoroughly, a little girl's voice can be silenced. In that moment, the silenced little girl in me finally reclaimed her voice."

Acknowledging Shame Takes Courage and Faith

Our bodies carry our shame. I see it when people walk into my office. I see it in their rounded shoulders, collapsed chests, and tucked pelvises. I see it in their lackluster eyes that avoid eye contact. I hear it in their monotone voices as they complain about their body pains, their spouses, their lives. Shame steals their joy, but they don't know it.

A good way to invite shame into our awareness is to set an intention. Experiment with saying, "I'm willing to say yes to any shame that may be stuck in my body." Acknowledge it. Welcome it. Witness it from your Being Self without judging it as bad. In fact, take a few moments to love your shame. That is, lie down, close your eyes, notice where you feel the shame in your body, and whisper to yourself, "I love myself for feeling shame, and for being brave enough to invite it into my awareness." Surround the shame with the same loving feelings you bring to your lover or child or adorable pet.

We can use shame as a gateway to joy if we're willing to feel it and love it. The moment we say yes to it, witness our shame with loving eyes, and respond to it with compassion, that is the moment we reconnect with our pure joy of Being. Why wait?

Practice Tools:

1. Find a quiet moment to invite any shame in your body into your awareness. Lie on your bed, sit under a tree, or lie on a soft blanket on the floor. Close your eyes. Take some long, deep breaths. With willingness and curiosity, whisper to yourself, "I'm willing to notice any shame in my body that I have been unwilling to notice." Just breathe in your belly and listen patiently for whatever bubbles up into your awareness. If you have been experiencing chronic pain in your body, focus directly on that area and ask, "Is this symptom related to shame?" Be willing to wonder, because this accesses your inner wisdom. The answer may arrive as a feeling sense, word or phrase, or an image or memory.

2. If you identify some shame, or suspect it without being able to pin it down exactly, lie on your back and locate where you sense the shame in your body. Breathe yes into it over and over. Let the yes ride your breath. As you stop resisting shame by saying yes to it, you allow it to come out of hiding and show its face. Now focus on the place the shame lives in your body and softly ask, "What is asking for acceptance here? What did I previously reject that is asking for

love and acceptance here?" Ask, take some deep breaths, let go of any thoughts or judgments, and just listen. Be open to whatever bubbles up.

3. Love yourself for feeling shame. Picture yourself letting waves of love wash over your body, and your shame, with each breath. Imagine a person or pet you really love, fill your body with that love, and shine it on your shame. All of our human experiences and feelings are here to be witnessed and loved by our nurturing, kind, accepting compassion, even our shame.

Mind Habits

In our normal way of life, we let ourselves be
controlled by powerful thoughts and emotions,
which in turn give rise to negative states of mind.
—HIS HOLINESS THE FOURTEENTH DALAI LAMA

WE SPEND MOST OF OUR LIVES LISTENING TO OUR MINDS.
Thoughts occupy much of our waking awareness. We busy ourselves
with planning personal and professional events. We reminisce about or
regret past moments, and fantasize future possibilities. We judge and
doubt ourselves and others. We make up stories to justify important
decisions. Some of these prove vital to making our lives function. But
these habits of mind come with a shadow side, too. These unconscious
mind habits evolved as ways for our less mature ego selves to survive.
In their naked truth, they are no more than clever ways that fear manufactured to prevent us from experiencing life, and feelings, directly. And
they come with a high price tag. They stop us from hearing the wisdom
of our bodies and our hearts.

In this section, I invite you to get to know your mind habits, especially their shadow side, much more intimately. I encourage you to help
your mind shift allegiance from serving fear to serving your heart. Let
this incredible tool called mind carry you below thoughts and plans,
doubts and judgments, into the deep untapped reservoir of inner
wisdom. Let mind become your heart's good friend. Instead of pulling
you out of the present, let mind help you stand fully in this present
moment. Let mind reassure you that you are safe as you honor your
feelings and surrender fully to your body's healing river of wisdom.
Teach mind to help you hear the soft whisper of your heart's longings.
As you ask your inner wisdom for guidance and wait patiently for
answers, mind becomes a skillful ally in shifting your identity into your
powerful, creative Being Self.

Obsessive Thinking and Worry

*Rather than distracting yourself with
thoughts and concepts, listen to your inner
voice, and you will find yourself
becoming much more relaxed and joyful.*
—TARTHANG TULKU

W hen I was twenty-five years old, the Tibetan Buddhist teacher Tarthang Tulku gave me an invaluable gift I have never forgotten. A simple tool for life. It was the mid-seventies in Berkeley, California. An older friend of mine from Mill Valley had invited me to the Sunday afternoon meditation. Whenever anyone suggested that I try meditation, I'd quip, "I do meditate. I meditate when I run." But that Sunday afternoon, sitting cross-legged with my eyes half-closed in the dimly lit, windowless basement of an ex-fraternity house on the University of California Berkeley campus, I learned something very important.

Tarthang Tulku offered the simple instruction to sit quietly, eyes half-closed, and watch my breath. I had great difficulty focusing. My mind wandered everywhere. I had just never watched it wander before. I thought about what wild fraternity parties must have taken place in that basement before it became the Nyingma Institute. That reminded me that I nearly lost my virginity in a fraternity house on the University of Oregon campus. Which started me thinking about my old boyfriend John, and whether I should have "gone all the way" with him at sixteen. Which triggered thoughts about my ex-husband, and why he left. My mind dragged me all over the place.

After forty-five minutes of struggling to watch my breath and failing miserably, the robust, black-haired man sitting cross-legged on a zafu in the center of the room rang a bell, signaling the end of meditation, and began to speak in his strange Tibetan accent. I felt drawn in by his sheer happiness. He looked happier than anyone I'd ever met in my life. And yet he was a refugee in a foreign country who had recently escaped terrorist Chinese rule over his beloved homeland. Still learning English, his words arrived brief and poignant. "Label thoughts, 'thinking, thinking,'" he taught, "let them go." I'd never seriously considered *not* listening to my mind before. (Remember, this was the mid-seventies, when self-help was still in the womb stage.)

Until that moment, I had always assumed that my mind was my best shot at moving cleverly through life. After all, it got me through college and landed me my prestigious journalism job in the Bay Area. But in that moment, he gave me the gift of freedom. Freedom to discover a me underneath my thoughts. I felt indescribably unhooked.

Later that day, I received a private ten-minute session with Tarthang Tulku. He said many things that I've since forgotten. But one thing stuck with me all these years. He looked right through me with his gentle, smiling face and radiant eyes, and said, "Much less small talk. Much less thinking. Then you be very good." I've recalled that gift in moments of despair, in times of fear and transitions, and on quiet walks in nature.

Our minds think and worry incessantly. That's just what minds do. Until we slow down and actually watch this thinking process for five minutes, or twenty, or forty-five, it's hard to comprehend how wildly they flit around from future plans to past memories and regrets to fears and fantasies, all in a few seconds. They constantly edit, critique, analyze, judge, and doubt our words, our actions, and our lives. Left to these old unconscious ways, minds habitually find things to obsess and worry about. They plan incessantly—our next weekend, our next vacation, our next drinking or food binge, our next money-making scheme—whatever today's current obsession is. The moment mind sniffs pain, discomfort, or emptiness in our bodies, it jumps into a wild fantasy of a better lover, better time, better job—anything to avoid the uncomfortable feelings underneath. In a nanosecond, the mind can daydream us onto a Caribbean island or have us dying from cancer before we even get our diagnostic test results.

Meditation doesn't stop the incessant thinking. It helps us put some breathing room around our thoughts. It helps us *choose* which thoughts we want to respond to, and how we want to respond to them. It reminds us each moment that our Being Self, and our capacity for joy, is much broader and more spacious than whatever thoughts happen to be running through our minds. It reminds us that we can simply be amused by our thoughts.

Labeling Our Thoughts Gives Us Freedom

Nothing could be simpler than labeling our thoughts, "thinking, thinking." Nothing could be easier than labeling our worries, "worrying, worrying." But this simple act can spell freedom. Freedom to stand in the moment, fully present. Freedom to see, hear, touch, smell, and experience life directly. Freedom to trust the process of life.

The mind is like a radio station. We can tune in to which thoughts are moving through us now. If we don't like this kind of music, if this station is filled with doubt or judgment or fear, we can label it, let it go, and change the station. We can switch to focusing on what our hands are touching, what our eyes are seeing, what our ears are hearing. The same way you might turn off country-western and tune in to classical or jazz.

Whether meditation is your thing or not, whether Buddhism turns you on or off, the simple act of labeling thoughts, "thinking, thinking" and worries, "worrying, worrying" is a Godsend. It can be used anytime, anywhere, without anybody else even knowing.

For example, Rick reached adulthood during the seventies. He manifested his dream life by using positive thinking. He ran a successful business. He took four months off every winter to ski (and sleep in). The other eight months he trained for triathlons after work. He loved being right. But when his midlife crisis hit, positive thinking failed miserably against his battle with depression.

Some of my tools failed, too. Exaggerating his depression and breathing directly into his feelings took us nowhere. One day I asked him when he most often felt most depressed. "At work," he replied. "I get so frustrated with my employees, I could scream. Plus my clients think I can talk all day. Yesterday I got totally bummed out, knowing that I'd have to spend an hour after work getting my wife's bike ready to ride before I could train. I was depressed by noon, just thinking about it."

Toward the end of the session, I said, "How about this. Whenever you catch yourself getting pulled down by your thoughts this week, would you be willing to label them, 'thinking, thinking' and let the thoughts go? Don't let them finish their sentence in your head. Label them and let them go. Then focus on what your eyes are seeing and your ears are hearing." He shrugged and nodded on his way out, mumbling, "Yeah, whatever."

The next week, he arrived with a curious grin on his face. "I've never been into meditation," Rick said. "I tried it, you know, years ago, but it was never my thing. Yet every time I caught myself thinking, I labeled it and came back into the present. Since I work outdoors, I looked up at the red rock cliff towering over my right shoulder, and I'd tune in to the crows cawing. The depression lost its grip." He had found the right tool for him, and now he knew how to stop his mind mid-sentence from bringing him down.

"Thinking, thinking" is the big umbrella label that covers everything. Rather than struggling inside with whether a thought is a worry, doubt, judgment, fear, memory, regret, or plan, it's easier to just label it, "thinking, thinking" and come back to our breath. It does the job, which is bringing us back into the present to experience life directly.

My own mind can get carried away obsessing about some insurance company holding up payment for therapy or the absurdity of wolves being legally shot from planes in Alaska, but the instant I notice it, I label it, "thinking, thinking." Suddenly, I'm back in the present— seeing the ponderosa pine I'm walking by, or hearing the Canada geese squawk overhead as they migrate. Labeling our thoughts can be a magic potion. It helps us take ourselves less seriously. It puts space between us and whatever is upsetting us. It has the power to move us from "totally caught up" to "light and flexible" in one second.

So why would anyone worry and obsess when we could be hanging out in joy? Because it's a habit. A deeply ingrained habit, which has been part of our human conditioning for centuries. And thinking serves fear, and our small ego selves, by preventing us from experiencing life directly. It also prevents us from feeling our joy.

Letting Ourselves Experience Life Directly

If we are busy thinking, thinking, we're not feeling, feeling. And that's the whole goal of losing ourselves in thought. When we want to avoid hurt, sadness, grief, fear, and anger (which for most of us is most of the time), this can feel like a huge bonus. A great perk. We learn this early on. When we are young, the intensity of many feelings can overwhelm us, or they may not be received well by our parents. Children quickly discover that, by breathing very shallowly, they can make those icky feelings disappear. To escape such unbearable feelings as intense loneliness or unworthiness, we learn to shut off from the neck down and "think" instead.

Like alcohol, thinking does temporarily remove the pain and discomfort. But, also like alcohol, the problem persists. To children figuring out how to survive and earn parental love, stifling their feelings, or abandoning their joy and aliveness, seems like a small price. But as we mature, this price becomes unbearable. Let's explore an example.

Frank came to see me. "What would you like to work on today?" I asked.

He said immediately, "My hypochondria! I woke up with a scratch on my nose yesterday morning," the thirty-eight-year-old husband and father said. "All of a sudden, in my mind, I have skin cancer. I'm convinced that I have skin cancer. I run to the doctor immediately to have it checked. While I'm in the waiting room, I remember that my grandfather died at age forty-eight. I tell myself that I, too, will probably die before I'm fifty. I'll never get to see my son grow up. I'll never see my grandchildren. By the time the doctor saw me, she was much more concerned about my anxiety than the scratch on my nose."

I asked Frank what his payoff was for obsessing. He shook his head. "None. There's no payoff." But after thinking about it, he said, "Maybe it keeps me from being present, from enjoying my life and my eleven-month-old son. When my wife and I get along great, like we are, it scares me." He sighed. He made a commitment to label his thoughts, "thinking, thinking" and try to allow more joy in his life. "I'm anxious about being a good father, but I guess I'll just feel the anxiety and quit making up stories."

None of us choose to abandon our joy. None of us wake up in the morning, saying, "Today I'll worry obsessively because it's too uncomfortable to hang out in joy." No. In fact, if anyone outright asked us, "Would you rather spend your day in joy or obsessive thinking?" we would all pick joy in a heartbeat. But it's habit. An unconscious habit that goes on below our awareness, as it has in human beings for centuries.

Experience the Unexpressed Feelings Underneath

So how do we stop? By witnessing the obsessive thinking or worrying, labeling it, and identifying the feeling underneath. All we need do is ask ourselves, "I wonder what feeling is fueling these thoughts?" Our inner wisdom is happy to answer.

For example, Mark suffered from chronic back pain. He had seen every neck, back, and nerve specialist in the area, but with little relief. In moments when his pain intensified, he worried obsessively: "Am I stuck with this pain the rest of my life?" "Will I be paralyzed?" "Will I ever be able to work again?" "Can I make love without damaging it more?" On and on. His mind created scenario after worst-case scenario.

When he repeated these thoughts out loud in my office, I smiled. "Ahhh," I injected. "Doesn't our mind have a fabulous imagination?" I asked him to label his fear thoughts, but this barely dented the constant flow of gloom and doom running through his mind. Then I asked if he would be willing to do the one thing he had been avoiding most.

"Would you be willing to feel whatever stuck feeling is fueling all these thoughts?"

He looked perplexed, so I explained. "There is the physical pain you feel in your body, which actually changes in intensity from moment to moment. Then there is all the angst and fear your mind brings to the actual sensation of pain. Would you be willing to focus directly on the pain and open to what feeling lives there?" He nodded.

Mark closed his eyes and took some deep breaths. "Now focus your attention directly on the pain. Imagine exhaling right down into the center of the pain." Tears streamed down his cheeks. "I'm so scared, Carolyn," he said. "I'm terrified I'll be stuck this way forever." "Yes," I responded softly, "really feel how scared you are."

"Oh, my god," he exclaimed. "I just tuned in to my pain, after I let all that sadness go, and my pain has actually lessened. It's still there, but it's less intense. And somehow I feel like I can handle it now without freaking out."

Mark had shifted his relationship to his pain and fear. He had responded with compassion.

We always have the choice, to let our thoughts keep dragging us around by the nose, or to label them, let them go, and respond to the feelings underneath with compassion. As we let them go, we touch our Being Self and the spaciousness of our unlimited joy.

Practice Tools:

1. This week, set an intention to get to know your mind. Whenever you notice yourself lost in thoughts, label it, "thinking, thinking" and gently bring your awareness back into the present. Focus on the in and out of your breath, and what your eyes are seeing, or your ears are hearing. Whenever you notice yourself obsessively worrying, label it, "worrying, worrying" and come back to the present. Whether brushing your teeth, driving your car, changing a diaper, working, or sitting down to eat, notice whatever thoughts are present, label them, and let them go. Then say, "In this moment, I choose joy." Don't feel obligated to let them finish their sentence. See how you feel inside as you keep choosing joy—no matter what happens around you. Hold your present experience in joy and love.

2. Practice experiencing life directly. Set an intention each morning this week, "I am willing to experience and feel life directly today." When you notice thoughts pulling you out of the present, running

a story, or keeping you lost in concepts, label it, "thinking, thinking" or, "worrying, worrying" and return to the present to experience what is. If you are afraid, notice how fear feels in your body. Locate where you feel it inside and describe the sensations of fear. If you feel sad, really be with the sadness, all the way. Don't postpone it or figure out *why* you are sad. Just be with it. When we open and experience feelings directly, they are much easier to handle than our mind (fear) tries to tell us. An instant way to bring yourself into the present is to ask yourself, "Am I here now?"

3. Experiment with expressing the feelings that are fueling your obsessive thoughts. Next time you catch yourself worrying about anything—money, love or lack of it, terrorism, health—close your eyes, take several deep breaths in your belly, and ask your heart, "What feeling is fueling this worry now?" Ask, breathe deeply, and patiently listen for a word or feeling sense to enter your awareness. Worry is often triggered by anxiety about some future event, especially if it feels out of our control. Fantasy is a common way we unconsciously jump into to avoid pain and emptiness inside. Discover which feelings fuel your worry thoughts. As you allow your Being Self to love and accept the worries, and the feelings fueling them, the need to obsess about anything quietly goes away.

Getting to Know ...

Planning Mind

Stillness of mind is enlightenment.
—H. W. L. POONJA

Planning is an integral part of our lives and our success. We plan our careers, our futures, our retirement. We plan our marriages, families, and homes. All the dreams we manifest in life begin with a plan. We plan fun weekends, exotic vacations, and trips to Europe or Africa to witness human history for ourselves. This world would fall into chaos without our elaborate, detailed planning. To avoid "wasting" time, we schedule every minute, every hour, every day in our Daily Planners long before we enter that moment.

I feel out of breath just thinking about what we do to ourselves: Meditate 5:45 to 6:15 A.M. Quick healthy breakfast. Drive children to school at 7:40 A.M. Treadmill and workout 7 to 8:30 Mondays, Wednesdays, and Fridays. Pilates or Spinner class, 7:30 to 8:30 Tuesdays and Thursdays. Arrive at the office by 9 A.M. Power lunch with a potentially huge client. Board meeting 1:10 to 2:55. Paperwork 3 to 4:30. Massage 4:45 to 5:45. Dinner at 6 with a friend. Meeting from 7:30 to 10 P.M. Power sleep 11-ish P.M. to 5:30 A.M.

We strive to make our first million by thirty-five, take up scuba diving and rock climbing on weekends, and begin high-elevation training for that Himalayan trek that will mark our fortieth birthday. Did I forget to mention remodeling the house in our spare time to maximize its resale value when we plan to sell in two years?

Planning Is a Foolproof Way to Avoid Feelings

Of course, planning is necessary. But when we are so busy planning the future that we repeatedly rob ourselves of the present moment, something's got to give. And by our forties or fifties, it does in the form of a heart attack or life-stopping illness. We often stay stuck in planning gear to avoid uncomfortable feelings. Like fear, plans promise us fun moments, promise relief from despair and depression, promise to hold boredom and loneliness at bay. But also like fear, plans promise a lot more than they can deliver.

We don't have to wait for illness, divorce, or trauma to drop this obsession with overplanning our lives. We can start now by getting to know our unconscious habit of planning better.

Buddhism teaches how plans distract us from the present moment by always pulling our focus into the future—a future reality that doesn't exist yet, except in our minds. They encourage us to label such thoughts, "planning, planning" and come back into the present. Psychologists warn that obsessive planning is most often fueled by anxiety, and encourage us to stop and learn how to cope with anxiety.

I encourage both: labeling thoughts, "planning, planning" whenever we notice them is a quick, handy way to pull ourselves back into the present. We will still make plans. But labeling helps us differentiate between healthy planning and compulsive planning in order to avoid feelings or hanging out in the unknown. Second, as we get to know the anxiety fueling our obsessive planning, the preoccupation with planning begins to fall away. Besides, obsessive planning only postpones the inevitable. After the exciting weekend is over, or the endorphins wear off, or the fabulous trip to Italy and France comes to an end, those uncomfortable feelings are still waiting for us in the quiet hush of our inner world.

Our planning mind doesn't stop planning just because we recognize it. Plans just keep rolling in. What changes is how we respond and how long we let our future plans hold us out of the present. As we *witness* plans, we choose to spend two minutes rather than two hours with whatever plan is in our awareness. If it's just an avoidance habit, we can choose to label it, "planning, planning," let it go, and step into the present.

Obsessive planning is often fueled by some unconscious belief such as not feeling good enough or not deserving love. If we allow time for spontaneous open space as well as plans, we can accomplish the same things in a much more relaxed manner. And the whole time, we can remind ourselves, "I am good enough."

Expanding Our Belief about Time

By rushing through our busy days, we tell our Inner Selves that we don't have enough time to do all the things we need to do. Like any belief, we can change this belief in an instant. When we notice our blood pressure rise at the prospect that there is not enough time to get it all done, we can respond to this old belief, and the accompanying anxiety, with loving compassion. We don't have to buy into it. We can take a deep breath and tell ourselves, "I have plenty of time. I deserve to care for my needs."

We can also shift our relationship with time by taking a few moments each day to pause and cultivate unconditional love toward ourselves. When we take fifteen minutes to lie down, close our eyes, take deep breaths, and check inside our bodies, we take time to listen to our needs and feelings and honor the wisdom of our inner voice.

When we say yes to whatever we are feeling inside—the fear, doubt, judgment, resentment, and shame that we have previously rejected— we don't have to run away anymore into planning mind. We relax with what is, and hold it in the compassionate love that lives in our core. This gives us more long-lasting joy than any plan.

Unstructured, open time is healthy for us. Healthy for our souls. It's one thing we give ourselves when we attend a meditation retreat or health resort. But it's important to remember that time is something *we can give ourselves in our own home.*

I stumbled upon the gift of unstructured time on vacation in southern Mexico in 1990. I had traveled there before but tended to fill each day with running on the beach, deep-sea fishing, nonstop reading, and riding the air-conditioned taxi to the jungle for bird-watching tours. Somehow, in 1990, I got it. I left my running shoes at home. I brought only my bikini, beach towel, sunglasses, journal, and four books. I stayed three weeks. The first week I spent unwinding from "city mind." I walked two hours on the beach every morning, swam in the crystal-blue ocean, read, napped, read some more, napped some more, made love, ate fresh fish and papayas, and played Uno.

But halfway through the second week, the sand and the ocean waves and the slow pace did their number on me. A voice inside said, "Put the book down. Just be here." I dropped into the moment, as if it was palpable, as if it was a real place to hang out. I watched waves rolling in without worrying about "wasting time." I felt how reassuring the constant roar of the waves had grown. I watched pelicans swoop low and surf the breeze just inches above the top of some treacherous, twenty-foot wave. I watched and watched the waves until, suddenly, I caught the dark outline of a large manta ray being carried up and up by the huge wave, then disappear. I looked more closely. More manta rays became visible to my naked eye, surfing the inside of the waves. Toward sunset, I watched as thirty-some pelicans flew out to sea in one, long, V-shaped formation.

I didn't want to leave this present moment, rich with magic, and go back to reading my book, or following some "plan" in my head. The challenge in daily life is to remember the magic amidst the busyness of clients, writing, relationship, and plans.

I invite you to drop below the plan now. Pause and feel the magic of this moment. Really hear the birds singing outside your window, or notice the inside of a raindrop or snowflake. Really see the color of the sky and try to name what color blue the sky is today, or what shape the clouds are painting in the sky. Lean back and treasure the gifts of this moment. I promise, there'll be plenty of time to get the important things done.

Practice Tools:

1. Take fifteen minutes each day this week to get to know "planning mind." Close your eyes, take several deep breaths, and watch your thoughts. When you notice any future thought, which could be what you are going to do in the next second or ten years from now, label it, "planning, planning." Then, bring your awareness back to the present, focus on inhaling and exhaling your breath, or what your eyes are seeing, or your ears are hearing. Feel the spaciousness of the present moment.

2. Set an intention to notice the feelings underneath planning. That is, label it, "planning, planning," then ask yourself, "What is the feeling underneath, fueling these thoughts?" Deep breathe and listen for your inner wisdom to answer. Whether it's anxiety, guilt, shame, or fear, practice witnessing the feeling and holding it in unconditional love. The more you simply love the feeling, no matter what it is, the less you need to habitually jump out of the present to avoid it.

3. Set aside an hour each day for "unstructured time" or "spontaneous soul time." This is separate from exercise time, meditation time, and yoga or tai chi time. It means that you step into this hour without a clue of what your soul might choose to do. Ask your heart, "What sounds good? What am I longing to do that I haven't had time for?" Ask, listen, and enjoy. You may let your body move to music however it wants to in your living room. You may find yourself drawing, painting, or singing. You may lie on the couch with a good novel, or call a friend. You may choose to lie on a comfortable lounger on the deck and listen to birds. Do whatever sounds good in *this* moment.

Remembering

When you understand one thing through and
through, you understand everything . . .
The best way is to understand yourself, and then
you will understand everything.

—SHUNRYU SUZUKI

W hen our minds aren't absorbed in planning, worrying, judging, or doubting, they easily slide into the past. When they are not busy planning what to wear today, or tonight's dinner, or next weekend's activities, they are busy remembering. They like to chew on what we said five minutes ago during that little confrontation with our boss, or what we should have said. They like to reminisce about the seventies, or nineties, or sixties—about how life used to be, before the family moved, before the baby came, before the accident, before the divorce, secretly longing for that same happiness again. They gravitate toward "better times" when we felt madly in love, or right after the baby arrived, wishing to have just one day of that back again.

Remembering, of course, can be just a few seconds of harmless reminiscing. Or it can be a powerful trap that cripples us from creating what we want. Either way, it always pulls us out of the present. When and how the habit of remembering pops into our awareness is out of our control. It just happens. The smallest thing, or a word somebody says in conversation, or seeing a couple kiss on the sidewalk on Valentine's Day, can instantly bring us back to last weekend, or ten years ago. What *is* in our control is whether we are awake enough to recognize the habit, and how we respond to it.

Recently, with my mother's passing away, I have noticed my mind flooded with memories of her life and our life together. I thumbed through hundreds of family snapshots to create a photo collage for her memorial service, and those images kept appearing in my morning meditation all week: The 1939 black-and-white shot of her slender 5'8" frame standing prim and proper in a white-collared, short-sleeved dress at her high school graduation. Mom in her early twenties in the saddle of a bucking brown-and-white pinto (the electric kind you plugged a nickel into for a five-minute ride) in downtown Jackson, Wyoming. Mom, in a brunette bob, holding her first-born infant in 1947.

Mom squatting with my brother and me in front of our brand-new 1957, two-tone Ford station wagon. Her standing in front of her begonias and roses in full bloom. Mom and Dad in front of the three-bedroom, ranch-style home they built in 1958. I remembered things I hadn't thought of for years, like fresh-baked apple crisp, roast turkeys, pumpkin pies, and the Christmas we were carried by horse and sleigh to Uncle Nelius' wildlife refuge because the roads were snowed in. This kind of reminiscing is appropriate, and harmless, around the time of someone's death. But not all of our remembering is harmless. The truth is, we disempower ourselves when we stay lost in memories, and regrets, for months or years.

Remembering Pulls Us Out of the Present

Too often, we hide behind memories to avoid the present. Too often, we use them to avoid uncomfortable feelings, or addressing an issue directly. We reminisce about how good our relationship "used to be" rather than creating the relationship we want now. We play victim by complaining about the past rather than empowering ourselves to act now. Too often, we hang out in the past far too long, or for all the wrong reasons.

When we are so focused on remembering how it was, we can't see how it is. When our minds are filled with memories, resentments, and regrets, there is no room for gratitude and appreciation. As we say yes to what is, we stop staying lost in what was. By witnessing our past memories, we empower ourselves to state our needs directly in the present. When we step into present time and share our vulnerable feelings, we stop hearing the voice that admonishes us to give up because it never worked in the past.

The quickest way out of memory lane is to label those thoughts, "remembering, remembering" and let them go. (After all, memory lane is never very accurate anyway.) Recognizing and labeling memories allows us to spend two seconds with them rather than two hours or two years. It frees us to open our hearts and feel all the love, joy, and abundance in the present moment. Many times, we are up to our necks in grace. But our habit of hanging out in past regrets blocks us from seeing it, or letting it in fully.

Creating What We Want Now

Returning to inner joy requires that we take full responsibility in the present. It invites us to access the wisdom of our Being Self by asking a few simple questions: "How am I *stealing my joy away* right now? What *unexpressed feeling* is triggering these repeated memories? What *quality* am I missing in my present life that these memories keep bringing my attention to? What hurt feelings do I need to talk about and forgive that keep triggering my memories? Am I willing to trust again, even if my trust was broken?"

As we come to know our own humanness better, we come to realize that people will hurt, disappoint, reject, and betray us on this journey. Those who love us the most, and spend the most time with us, can hurt us the most. The only thing we can control is how we respond. Bottom line, the important question to ask in response to whatever happens is: "How am I reacting to this, and how am I stealing my joy away right now by my reaction?"

Tom and Sharon came to couple's therapy last week. Sharon cried almost immediately. "Here, read this," she said as she shoved a folded piece of white paper into my hand. "You'll see that Tom isn't the glowing angel he makes himself out to be in here."

I read the letter out loud to them. "The first few years together," Tom had written, "you used to be so caring, sensitive, and kind to me. That's the Sharon I fell in love with. But you're always too busy with work and exercise and meetings to be there for me. I drive the kids to school, I prepare dinner for the family after work, I weed and water all the flowers, I bring you nice presents just to show I love you, and you don't give much back. You're so selfish and absorbed in yourself all the time, such a narcissist. All the time, I catch myself remembering how it used to be, how you used to be with me. I need you to go to therapy, I need you to change or I'm getting a divorce." Tom looked out the window in silence. Sharon held her head in her hands, crying.

"These are some strong words, Tom," I reflected. "It sounds like you spend a good deal of time remembering the past. Would you be willing to turn your complaints into a request?" He shrugged. "It won't do any good," he mumbled.

"We don't know if it will do any good, but would you be willing to try?" I asked. "And are you willing to drop the 'D' word, because that's such a power play, it pulls the rug out from under Sharon's feet and disables her from giving you what you need?"

Tom reluctantly agreed to tell Sharon how hurt he felt and state his needs directly to Sharon. He took Sharon's hands, looked her in the eye, and said, "I'm so scared about my knee surgery next week, much more nervous about it than I let on. And I've been really hurt these past few months that you just went about your business as usual, never once offering to drive me to the hospital, be there for me when I woke up out of surgery, or drive me home. Several of my friends are clamoring to do those things, which hurt even more that you didn't offer. I need you to take the day off from work."

"Of course, Tom," she jumped in. "I asked you earlier, but you said you'd taken care of it and didn't need me. I'm happy to take off work and be there for you."

Over the next several months, Tom became skilled at witnessing his tendency to play victim by hiding in past memories. When he caught himself reminiscing about the "good old days," he asked himself, "What needs do I need to ask directly of Sharon?" As Sharon became more attentive, he felt safer to talk about his memories with her rather than letting them fuel his resentment. The "D" word stopped coming up.

Our young ego self loves to hang out in memories—or anything else to avoid feeling vulnerable. When we buy into it, our needs stay unmet, simply proving the old fears and beliefs right. It's our responsibility to state our needs clearly in order to optimize our chances of getting our needs met. And it's our responsibility to change complaints into requests, then give loved ones the breathing room to say no when they need to.

Responding to Memories with Compassion

It's challenging to stay in the present. Experienced meditators will be among the first to tell you that, despite years of labeling memories and letting them go, their minds continue to lodge themselves in past memories, future fantasy, self-judgment, doubt, and fear. It is the nature of mind—to bounce around wildly, vying for our attention. Our job is to be awake enough to notice memories when they are passing through, label them, and hold our young ego self in compassion.

We all have memories of the great love that got away, the valuable piece of property we let slip through our fingers, or the moment we'd like to do over again. But at some point, we have to take responsibility for our choices. We have to appreciate the life we chose, even though it never quite matches the fantasy. At some point, we need to let ourselves off the hook, relax into what is true, and trust what is.

If I learned one thing from reminiscing about my mother's life after she died, it is that life really is short, much shorter than we ever think. Meditation teacher Stephen Levine once said, "Life is like a long weekend." We do what we do, we choose to spend our time reminiscing about the past or experiencing life directly in the present, and then we die. The big, final goodbye comes either way. There is only this moment, and how present we are to respond to it. So why wait? Begin today cultivating your relationship with your powerful Being Self, and hold your memories in loving compassion and joy.

Practice Tools:

1. Set an intention to notice whenever your mind is hanging out in the past (anywhere from one second ago to your earliest childhood memory). Whenever you notice it, label it, "remembering, remembering," then let it go. You have no obligation to let it finish its sentence. Label it in a neutral tone, without judgment. Then focus in the present, noticing what you are seeing, touching, or hearing.

2. Witness your memories by noticing how they feel in your body. What feeling does this memory trigger? What stuck feelings live underneath the memory, fueling it? (Often anger, fear, sadness, resentment, or grief can trigger us to reminisce about a happier time in the past.) As you really feel the feeling fueling the memory, this empowers you to take action in the present.

3. Set aside twenty minutes to connect with your Being Self. Lie down on a comfortable bed or sofa with a pillow under your knees, taking several deep breaths in your belly, and focus your attention on whatever sensations you notice in your shoulders, arms, and hands. Then shift to noticing any sensations in your legs and feet. After grounding yourself by doing this for a few moments, focus on your torso, noticing any feelings or longings present. From your Being Self, send compassion to your young ego self that is feeling lonely, or sad, or longing for a time in the past when things felt easier. Don't buy into the past memory. Just be compassionate for the part of you that is hurting in this moment. Ask your wise Being Self, "What *feeling quality* is missing from my life right now that brings me to this past memory?" Once you identify it, ask, "How might I bring this quality into my present life?" (Whether it's wanting to belong, wanting to feel more visible and cared about, or more loved and accepted, asking questions helps access our inner wisdom.) Promise to take one step today toward bringing this into your life.

4. When you notice a particular memory coming back again and again, ask what unexpressed feeling is fueling this memory. Whether it is regret, emptiness, or grief, make time to express it. Then create time to *talk about* the memory, and its underlying feeling, with a loved one or good friend. Describe what it has been saying to you in your mind, how it feels in your body, and tell them clearly what you realize you need as a result of exploring it.

Getting to Know ...

Judgment

The most fundamental aggression to
ourselves . . . is to remain ignorant by not
having the courage and the respect
to look at ourselves honestly and gently.

—PEMA CHODRON

Life continually brings us surprises. As we wade through an unexpected illness, divorce, surgery, loss, or hurricane, we can easily feel robbed of joy. If we hold stubbornly to the idea that we can only feel joy when everything is pleasant, we cheat ourselves out of much inner joy that can be found in all situations. By judging everything as "good" or "bad," "pleasant" or "painful," we block our joy in the present.

To live in joy, we must learn to respond with openness and flexibility to the paradoxes in life. We must learn to stay afloat and balanced amidst surprises. This means examining our knee-jerk reactions to things we label as "bad" and acknowledging our habits. In other words, we have to come to terms with the joy-stealing judge inside.

Think about all the ways we listen to our judge everyday. The weather is *too* hot, *too* windy, *too* cold, *too* humid. We are *too* sensitive, *too* cowardly, *too* passive, *too* boisterous. Our lover is *too* shy, *too* passionate, *too* intellectual, *too* boring. We judge our fellow human beings as *too* pushy, *too* greedy, *too* arrogant, *too* weak. Everything is *too* something. That's the judge at work.

Self-judgment keeps running the same stories over and over. And for some reason, we keep listening: Am I rich enough? Sexy enough? Smart enough? Respected enough? Fit enough? Good enough? Have I done enough to satisfy my parents? The answer is always never. Not in the eyes of judgment. It could always be better. You could always do more. Even at the end, when we are dying, that judgmental voice inside scans our life and deems our accomplishments not good enough. It's time to respond differently to our inner judge, to stop listening. It's time to witness it for what it really is, harsh, cruel judgment, and stop wasting our precious time believing it.

Feeling Judged by Others

Usually, we make up our own judgments and project them onto others. For example, Laura and Rick came to me for couple's therapy. Laura had decided a few years back that Rick was unfeeling, incapable of being there for her feelings. She felt totally justified to "judge" him as failing her. After all, that felt safer than exposing her tender needs and risking rejection. Instead of speaking up, she jumped into fantasizing some conscious, strong, sensitive man coming along to sweep her off her feet. Rick needed help practicing his listening skills, but he was far from hopeless.

I invited them to stand up, face each other, and look into each other's eyes. I asked Rick if he was willing to hear Laura's feelings without interrupting her. "Imagine putting duct tape over your mouth, if you have to," I joked. He smiled and said, "OK."

I asked Laura to "witness" her judgments by owning them out loud to Rick. She looked chagrined. "Every day, I have thoughts about leaving you," she said. "My fear says that this time won't be any different than the last hundred. I'm afraid you won't listen to my feelings, or you'll take them personally and reject me." By now she was crying.

"Good," I said, recognizing that, with the tears, she had dropped into a very young, tender place. I softly encouraged, "Would you be willing to tell Rick how painful it is inside for you when your feelings did not feel received? Describe it."

Laura's body shifted nervously from side to side, showing how scary it was for her to directly reveal her vulnerable feelings. "Tell Rick your *whole* truth," I added, "which includes how scared you are to open your mouth right now and share." Tears streamed down her face as I rubbed her back softly. She moaned under her breath.

"It is so, so painful, so scary when you take my feelings personally and hear them as criticism. My whole body knots up. Part of me never wants to speak to you again," she said. "I just need you to *listen*. Just receive me. Just hear me. Don't do anything, don't fix anything, just *listen*. That's all I need. When I share my sadness, I feel five years old again and my dad is yelling at me for crying. You have to realize that I feel five inside and listen to me with the same tenderness you used with your five-year-old daughter. Just hold me, reassure me, and *listen*."

He heard her. From that moment on, Rick tried hard to listen to her feelings and not be defensive. Over the next several months, he fell back into taking things personally, then caught himself and apologized, saying he really wanted to hear her feelings. As he softened and listened, she began to trust him more with her tender-most feelings. It took time, as learning to trust often does, but eventually their relationship changed.

Meditation teacher Jack Kornfield said during a dharma talk that what most people want is to be listened to, acknowledged, honored, and heard from the heart and soul. We know this deep inside. Yet it seems to be a message we all need to keep hearing. We need to honor our own needs and feelings, and honor those of our loved ones.

Judging is a habit, a bad habit. It creates distance between our vulnerable, soft feelings and our ego selves. It creates distance between ourselves and the people we love most. It's the past conditioning that our parents, grandparents, and ancestors have unconsciously passed along to us for centuries. But it's not a habit we have to perpetuate, not once we get to know it better. Getting to know judgment, witnessing it chatter away at us inside our heads, is the quickest way to be free of it.

This change doesn't have to take years. If we spend ten minutes each day focusing inside and "listening" to what story our judge is replaying today, we can be amused by its yen for gossip. It's when we don't bother to know our own inner judge and "hear" what judgment sounds like that we stay imprisoned by its cruel, harsh messages.

Like fear, the inner judge has a great imagination. If allowed to, it finds fault in everybody. Given half a chance, it would even find fault with Jesus Christ and Buddha in a heartbeat. Because its job is to judge. To find the one thing wrong. To always point out how life could be better. Our job is to recognize it, label it, and let it go.

Recognizing When We Are Judging Ourselves

This habit of judging ourselves has various roots. Some of us grew up with a critical parent. Others picked it up in grade school by comparing themselves to other kids who had more confidence, better verbal skills, a new expensive toy, or some hot new outfit. It doesn't really matter where it came from, or how many years we've been at it. What matters is that we are, all of us, masters at judging ourselves. This habit is so deeply ingrained that we do it unconsciously, not realizing how cruel we are to ourselves. For example, with two growing children and a new business, Sam wanted to move out of his rebellious twenties and make more money. His father had invested several thousand dollars into his new business, and he felt pressure to "make it." But he kept feeling like everyone had been handed the key to success but him.

I suspected that his inner judge was blocking his success, so I had him stand in front of a full-length mirror and say out loud the things he told himself inside. "You idiot," he sneered, "what makes you think you can pull off a huge business like this? You've always played at work while daddy picked up the tab when money got tight. Your grandpa said you'd never be good at business, and he was right. You're a failure."

Halfway through, Sam started crying. "I had no idea how cruel I was being until I heard the words out loud," he said. I encouraged him to spend the next several weeks labeling his judgments, "judging, judging" and letting them go. Then I asked, "What would your Inner Self, who is working twelve-hour days, like to hear?"

He paused a moment. "I'd love to hear what I'm doing right." A few months later, his new business was featured on the cover of a trade journal. His mind stepped aside and allowed success.

It's always easier to hear how cruel someone else's judgments are than to recognize our own. We judge ourselves all the time for feeling too sad, or we jive ourselves for feeling afraid when we shouldn't be afraid. Though we seldom see this as judgment. By labeling all our judgmental thoughts as "judging, judging" and letting them go, however, we prick the big all-consuming judgment balloon—and it deflates quickly. By labeling it, "judging, judging," we no longer identify with our young ego self who is doing the judging unconsciously, out of habit. Instead, we identify with our mature Being Self, who has only compassion for whatever judgments are flowing through us.

By seeing our judgments clearly, we also stop a habit that hurts our relationship: projecting our self-judgments onto those close to us. Our projections sound something like this: "*They* think my nose is too big, my breasts are too small, my hips are too large, my skin is too dark . . ." "*She* wishes I would be more sensitive." "*My clients* expected me to finish this last week." In other words, *we* make up a judgment in our heads, skip over recognizing it as our own, and project our own judgment onto someone outside of us. They might indeed think my nose is too big or my breasts are too small, but we don't really know what they are thinking until we ask. Meanwhile, we need to recognize our own judgments as projections—and see how we steal our joy in the process.

Since we are human beings with minds, we judge. Judgments don't stop just because we become skilled at recognizing, labeling, and letting them go. Judgments still come and go, moving in and out of our awareness. But judgments will create distance between ourselves and others, if we let them. They will close our hearts, if we let them. So it's important to witness our judgments as they pass through, and respond to them with compassion from our Being Self. Responding with compassion takes only a few moments, freeing us to spend hours basking in our unlimited joy that waits, like sunshine, for us to clear the clouds of judgment away.

Practice Tools:

1. Cultivate lots of nonjudgmental curiosity for this one. For one month, be willing to notice any and all ways you judge yourself. Even if you think you are so over judgment, see what comes up. Write down what you see, and learn. If you judge your looks, body shape, age, worldly success, sexual track record, driving history, and so forth, just jot down what you see.

2. After one month of witnessing your judgments, stand in front of a large mirror, look directly into your eyes, and read off all the judgments you wrote down. Notice how this feels in your body. (It's often tearfully painful.) Then close your eyes and ask your heart what it would like to hear from you. It may quietly say, "I need to know that I'm important" or, "I need to hear what I'm doing right." Just ask, take some deep breaths, and patiently listen for your Inner Self to respond.

3. When you notice a judgment, any judgment, say yes inside. Let yes ride the in and out of your breath. Label it, "judging, judging" and let it go, bringing your awareness back into the present moment, to what your eyes are seeing, your hands are touching. Notice how the judgment feels in your body. Notice which thoughts and stories it triggers. Ask, "What am I getting out of judging myself (or others) right now?"

4. Practice shifting your identity into your wise, mature Being Self. When you witness a judgment, close your eyes, take some deep breaths, and whisper to yourself, "I'm willing to respond to this judgment from my Being Self." Think of someone or something you naturally feel lots of compassion for, and shine that compassion onto the young part of you inside that is lost in judgment. Notice what feeling is underneath, fueling the judgment, and hold that in compassion. Love yourself for feeling judgmental, and love the feeling that fueled it.

Getting to Know...
Doubt

Most of us are dragged toward wholeness...
We cling to the familiar, refuse to make
necessary sacrifices, refuse to give up habitual
lives, resist our growth.
—MARION WOODMAN

Throughout our lives, self-doubt is a frequent visitor. In high school, we doubt our academic and athletic abilities, our sex appeal, and our ability to keep our boyfriend or girlfriend. In our twenties and thirties, we fret over careers, money, relationships, children, and who likes whom (most importantly, who likes me). By our forties and fifties, midlife hits, and we doubt our life choices—our choice of a mate, our decision to have children or not, and whether we chose the right career. Somewhere in there, we doubt whether we'll ever have enough for retirement, or whether we'll live long enough for retirement—is that hard lump malignant?

Doubt travels with us our entire lives, as familiar as a worn-out shoe. It's the insatiable critic inside forever raising questions: Am I smart enough? Sexy enough? Rich enough? Thin enough? And with the human potential movement, we have new things to doubt: Am I practicing right livelihood? Am I living up to my potential, pursuing my soul's purpose? Is the person I love my soul mate? Will I ever find my soul mate? Does my spirit belong in the city or the country, the ocean or the mountains? And then there's the biggest doubt of all, circling our lives like a vulture: am I lovable? If we allow it, doubt drives a wedge between us and our wildest dreams. It shrinks our confidence and blocks us from trying new things, even love. Doubt runs as fast as it can away from life and love and joy, and it tries to drag us with it. Doubt fears change. Doubt fears being wrong. It fears making a mistake. Doubt is a wimp. It's the Chicken Little part of us that says, "Don't say that! Don't do that! The sky will fall!" Doubt's job is to slow us down and make us rethink things over and over. If we do, we stop our momentum. We leave a crack in the door for a big gust of fear's logic to blow us over.

We doubt. Because these human bodies arrive complete with complex minds, we doubt. Doubt questions everything: every thought, every action, every decision. Doubt knows no boundaries. It questions us *before*, *during*, and *after* we decide to take an action. The bigger the risk, the louder the doubt. So the best strategy is to expect it. Welcome it. Be amused by its imaginings. Just stop buying into it.

Especially when we are making big decisions, doubt arrives loud and lasts long. In the midst of a changing career, doubt asks: "But will you be able to pull off your new career? Can you make enough money at it to live on?" When our knees are shaking over a pending marriage or commitment ceremony, doubt has a heyday. "Are you *sure* this is Mr. (or Ms.) Right, or should you wait? Could you do better? Does he or she *really* love you, or are you just the rebound lover?" When facing divorce, doubt acts like our long-lost best friend. "Are you *sure* you dare go through with this? What if you end up alone the rest of your life? What if the next relationship is worse?" When we engage in a new creative project, doubt arrives like clockwork, perches itself in the front row, and critiques every performance to make us doubt and question every move. Count on it.

We doubt. No matter how successful we are in the outside world or how much money we have, we doubt. No matter how many years we meditate and study consciousness, we doubt. No matter how many self-help books we read, or how many fears we have conquered through sheer willpower, we doubt. Because doubt is not something we can exterminate. It just is. Our best defense is to get to know it.

In Western culture, our first defense is to eradicate problems, symptoms, diseases, anything in our way. But we can't cut out doubt the way we cut out organs when they give us problems. Doubt is deeply entrenched in our psyches. It's been part of our human conditioning for centuries. The key question then is, how can we get to know it?

Welcoming Doubt without Letting It Stop You

The most conscious thing you can do is become *very* familiar with the voice of doubt inside your mind. Get to know it really well. Recognize whether it is guilt-tripping you into feeling paralyzed, or seducing you with logic and reason. Discover for yourself which doubts you brush off easily, like an annoying fly, and which you get completely hooked by. Become familiar with how doubt sounds in your head and feels in your body.

Doubt doesn't only appear during big decisions. Every day, several times a day, doubt visits us. It questions what we say and do, and how we say and do it. "Why did you say *that*? You just made a total fool of yourself." "Don't bring up that heated issue with your spouse. Do you remember what happened last time? It will end in an argument, and then you'll regret it." Too often we believe doubt as gospel truth and make life decisions based on its lies. Sometimes we lie to ourselves and pretend we aren't doubting, we're just being smart (which usually means buying into the logical voice of fear). On the best days, we say yes to doubt, witness it, and chuckle at its absurd thinking.

When I became a writer, I needed to increase my knowledge of doubt. Doubt tried hard to sabotage my writing. Some days, it succeeded. My hands would be flying over the keys, when suddenly doubt would stop me cold. "You don't have anything new or important to say. Give it up! You're making a total fool of yourself. Go skiing or mountain biking—something you're good at."

At first, I believed it. I questioned what I was doing. But now (on good days) I recognize it, label it, "doubting, doubting" and let it go. I've grown to expect it in the mornings, when I'm meditating in preparation to write. "You should be writing, not indulging your selfish habit," it scolds. "Do you even have a clue what you'll write about today?" I smile. "Hello, doubt," I say. "How are you today? Full of yourself again, I see." After I'm done writing, there it is again, telling me I didn't write enough, or write well enough. My Being Self reassures my writer inside that she did a good job today.

Responding to Doubt with Kindness and Compassion

We learned how to spell doubt correctly in grade school, but not how to recognize it. Under the umbrella of right and wrong, we learned well how to frame life into two narrow categories: who's right, and who's wrong. But love and life are so much bigger than the tiny, narrow world of right and wrong. As we broaden our understanding of doubt, and life, it's important to step outside of that tiny right/wrong box. In fact, while you are at it, throw that tiny box right out the window. And take a few moments to replace doubt with unlimited joy, and love, and creativity. Responding to doubt with kindness and compassion is the key.

Clients rarely enter my office saying, "I'm struggling with doubt today. Can you please help me?" Instead, they arrive immersed in doubt, buying into it as real.

For example, for several months in therapy, Lisa explored her doubts about staying married. "I care deeply about Jack as a person, I love him," she said of the man she had lived with for twelve years. "But I'm not in love with him. After turning forty, it's not enough anymore. He's not enough." Even before therapy, she had been plagued with doubts about the marriage for four long years. Finally, she filed for divorce. She packed up her belongings and her cat, and moved to a tiny apartment.

Within two months, Lisa met a new lover. They traveled to Italy and France that summer. At the end of the trip, they moved in together. Lisa felt happier than she had ever felt. "Before therapy," she told me, "joy was never a big consideration in my life. I worked, kept my commitments, and trudged through. Now, joy is my guiding compass."

But in her last session with me, doubt reappeared. This time, however, she had practice recognizing it, and conscious tools for dealing with it. She knew how to relate to it from compassion. Instead of losing herself in doubt and asking me, "Did I make the right decision, Carolyn?" she taught me about it from her Being Self. "Right now some doubt is moving through me," she acknowledged. "It's asking me if I made a mistake. If I tried hard enough in my marriage. If I'll regret leaving five years from now. It's OK," she reassured her young self. "You can trust your decision. Just notice how happy you feel in your body and your heart. Trust your happiness. It's telling you the truth."

The more choices we have, the more room there is for doubt. These days, choices abound. Marriage is no longer forever. Careers only stick as long as they maintain our interest, or until our industry undergoes the latest wave of downsizing, or until we are laid off. We can live by the ocean, or in the mountains, or have homes in both places. With choices pulling us in every direction, we have to let our wise Being Selves help us discern between the doubt in our minds and the truth in our hearts.

Trust and Compassion Are the Antidotes for Doubt

As we witness and label doubt for what it is, we drop down into the spaciousness of Being—and discover doubt's opposite: trust. We begin to trust ourselves. Trust our decisions. Trust our hearts. Trust that we are having the experience we are supposed to be having. Trust that the person standing in front of us, saying he or she loves us, is speaking the truth. Trust life. Trust the Universe and the gifts it brings us.

From our wise Being Self, it's much easier to feel compassion for our younger self inside who had to rely on doubt to survive as a child. The next time doubt strikes, try loving your young ego self for doubting, without any judgment. Lead him or her by the hand over to the side of trust. Love what is. Love yourself for whatever is true in this moment.

Afterwards, fill the open space that arises with the unlimited joy and love that live in your heart. Listen for the soft, quiet voice inside that reminds you, "No matter what is happening around you, you are safe and you are loved." This is the loving voice of your Being Self. Ask it what you need and want. Bask in its loving compassion as often as you think of it. Then move on with the business of creating the life you want.

Practice Tools:

1. For one month, make a commitment to get to know doubt better. Each morning, say to yourself, "I'm willing to see clearly any ways doubt fills my awareness today." Become skilled at noticing what triggers it, how loud, soft, or seductive it sounds inside, how doubt feels in your body, and what feelings come with it. Notice how it affects your perception—of yourself, loved ones, and the world. When you notice it, label it, "doubting, doubting," and focus on the in and out of your breath in present time. If it bounces back in immediately, again label it, "doubting, doubting" and let it go. Be patient. The more you label it, the more it eventually becomes bored and loosens its tight hold on you.

2. Pick one of your major doubts and exaggerate it. If it sounds like, "I don't know if I want this relationship anymore" or, "I'm not sure I'm in the right work," set ten minutes aside, find a private room, and totally indulge your doubt. Say its thoughts out loud. Storm or stomp around the room being the voice of doubt to the hilt. Within minutes, you will be laughing heartily at it. But this makes it fully conscious so you can easily recognize and label it in your busy life.

3. When you notice a particular doubt repeatedly coming up, ask yourself, "What is the payoff I get for doubting myself around this?" Or another way to see the perks you get from it is to keep finishing this sentence: "As long as I keep doubting myself for _____, I don't have to _____ (risk failure, be vulnerable, enter the unknown, risk rejection, go after what I really want.)

4. Teach loved ones about your doubts rather than buying into them. That is, address doubt by telling your mate, "I notice some doubt bubbling up into my awareness right now. It's telling me to question your love for me, to not trust your words, to doubt your ability to care for my needs." Talking about your doubts saves your body from having to act them out and creates more intimacy.

5. Respond to doubt from your Being Self with loving compassion. To connect with your Being, lie down, take some deep breaths in your belly, and focus on whatever sensations you notice, first in your

arms, then in your legs. After a few moments, shift awareness to your torso. Notice any tension, pressure, sensations, or feelings present in your torso. Once you feel deeply connected with your Being Self, let it send loving compassion to the part of you inside that feels frozen by doubt. Continue to send loving compassion until the doubt dissipates and all you feel is a peaceful humming vibration throughout your body.

The Stories We Make Up

*Repeated thoughts and stories are
almost always fueled by an unacknowledged
emotion or feeling underneath.*

—JACK KORNFIELD

We all know the routine. Something happens to trigger our feelings of hurt, fear, disappointment, or rejection. And to save us from experiencing the raw emotions, our minds make up stories. Stories we believe. Stories that distract us, pull us out of the uncomfortable present moment. It's as if our mind keeps a special locked file cabinet in the basement filled with all our past hurts, disappointments, failures, and losses. As soon as our young ego self gets even a whiff of some approaching hurt, it dives into the files and dredges up some old story that worked last time. Bless its heart. It believes that if it can just preoccupy our awareness with stories, we won't feel so hurt.

We should give our young ego self credit. It's such a noble gesture. The problem is, we are in the habit of believing these stories. After all, we learned this well by listening to Mom and Dad's stories of blame and fear when we were toddlers, before we could discriminate. By the time we reached our twenties and thirties, and experienced our own pain and broken hearts, we added a few stories of our own to the file.

There is just one small problem. As long as our awareness is filled with stories, we can't experience life directly. We can't feel our joy. If we don't learn to respond differently, real life passes us by while we stay snagged by the stories in our head.

Some psychologists call these stories, "self-talk" or, "our inner critic." Buddhism refers to doubt, boredom, restlessness, lustful fantasies, fears, and jealousies as "demons." Whatever we call them, the important thing is noticing how we habitually talk to ourselves, nonstop. Our young ego self seems to have an editorial opinion about everything, which can quickly be embellished into a dramatic story. We listen politely. But when we stay preoccupied with these incessant stories, we can't hear the birds singing or the leaves rustling in the wind, or the soft, shy voice of our own hearts.

Becoming Familiar with Our Stories

It's critical to recognize our stories as stories, not the gospel truth. The first step is to say yes to whatever story is grabbing at our attention, then let it go.

When we believe our stories, what we are really listening to is the voice of fear. It may be couched in very reasonable, logical terms, but it's still fear. It takes the shape of an inner jukebox, playing our favorite oldies but goodies—the tapes we grew up with, or made up to protect ourselves from hurt. When rejection strikes, we instantly hear that old favorite, "The world really is a scary place," complete with flashbacks of past rejections. When we have a longing to forgive our lover for past hurts, the old tune, "Don't trust nobody" serenades us. And when we finally muster up the courage to leap into the unknown to create our dream, we hear, "Watch out! Life's full of disappointment."

But the truth is, we weren't born with this inner jukebox. We *learned* how to make up stories to protect our young ego selves, which means we can *unlearn* it. We are the ones who let these old stories drag us around by the nose, even if we do it unconsciously. And we have the ability to say yes, witness and label the stories, and let them go. It just takes a little attention. It just takes a few moments each day to develop a healthy relationship with our Inner Selves.

Saying Yes to the Story

When we say yes to the story racing in our minds, our resistance disappears.

We begin to shift identities from our young ego Wizard of Oz, behind the big machine, to our wise, mature Being Self. From this new perspective, we can witness the story with amusement as it falls apart. The story has now served a higher purpose: it has helped us "wake up" and shift into our Being Self. Another way to create this shift is to ask ourselves, "What unexpressed feeling is fueling this story line?" Rather than letting it build a strong case—which "story" is so adept at doing—we can use it as an opportunity to drop down inside and get to know ourselves better.

Next time you catch your mind running a story, no matter how elaborate and interesting (and reasonable) it sounds, try labeling it, "story, story" and letting it go.

For years, John dug through his old files and ran the same story through his head when he felt like an outsider in his family. "It's them, my wife and two daughters, against me. They don't care about my needs. Nobody cares if my feelings are hurt. They take what they want and leave me to clean up the mess." For years, he had only two reactions: to yell angrily or mope in his study. This occurred like clockwork on holidays.

When he came into therapy, he related his story to me. Only he didn't recognize it as a story. He believed he was telling me the facts. He explained that he felt like the odd man out. He felt ganged up on, misunderstood, pushed aside. Rather than buy into his story, as he had done, I asked him to exaggerate this position. He walked around my office, venting his frustration, saying everything he didn't dare say at home. At the end of the session, I invited him to treat it differently. "Next time you feel ganged up on," I said, "would you be willing to drop below the story line, and notice what you are feeling?"

He agreed. After the Christmas holiday, he returned. "You're not going to believe this, Carolyn," he said. "That 'left out' story started up on Christmas morning. I watched my wife hug our oldest for her gift, and boom, there it was again. I felt isolated. So instead of sulking and forcing them to ask me what's wrong, I quietly excused myself. I went into the bedroom, lay down, and asked inside, 'What feeling is fueling this?' I began to cry. I remembered feeling so unseen and misunderstood as a boy, and I saw for the first time how painful it was. When these same feelings were triggered by my family, I believed them rather than seeing that I had an opportunity to heal this old pain. I went back out to the living room and asked everyone to listen while I shared something.

"I described how the story got triggered when my wife hugged Angie, and what I discovered by exploring the feelings underneath. Then I told them what I needed. "If you see me withdraw as you have so many times, will you softly ask me what I'm feeling?"

They agreed. With practice, he began to notice the story line within moments of its arrival, witness it, and address his feelings and needs more directly. As his wife and daughters helped by asking him what he was feeling, he felt closer to them and more loved.

Getting Comfortable with the Raw Energy of Life

Day by day, year by year, our stories stop us from living our lives directly, if we let them. They try to convince us that the smart thing is to hide our silly dreams in our back pockets, or deep inside our hearts. They promise our Inner Self that *someday*, when it feels safer, easier, and more comfortable, then maybe we'll get to drag out those old dreams and dust them off. If we're not careful, stories will extinguish our passion, cover up our joy, and convince us that TV really is an adequate facsimile for life. We fantasize a happier, more exciting life while toking on a joint, sipping wine, or ingesting too many caramel-covered muffins when nobody is watching. Before long, we give up. When we finally look for the boisterous, go-for-broke self we used to be, it's nowhere to be found.

It's our job to witness our favorite stories (as attached as we are to some of them) and let them go. It's our job to drop below the story line and face our raw feelings. When we were young, dependent, and less mature, we had to make up stories. But as mature adults, we need to replace those "oldie but goodie" stories with receiving life directly.

Old stories provide us with plenty of logical reasons to never trust again, never love again, never open our hearts again, never be vulnerable again. But we have to resist our temptation to buy into them and limit ourselves to the voice of fear, couched in reason. I routinely tell my clients, "You have a *perfectly good reason* to close your heart. You were hurt, devastated, abandoned, or neglected by someone you thought loved you. But what is your choice? To keep your heart closed by letting fear convince you that any person standing in front of you, loving you, is untrustworthy? Or to open your heart, even though you risk being hurt and disappointed again?" When it's put so bluntly, most of us drop the reasonable story and choose to open our hearts. It's the doorway marked *compassion*.

A sign sits at each trailhead in Rocky Mountain National Park, near Estes Park. It reads: "Remember: the mountains don't care." It warns novice adventurers to always carry water, waterproof jackets, extra food, a flashlight, sturdy boots, and a first aid kit, even on days when the sky looks cloudless and sunny at the trailhead. That's because weather in the Rockies has the reputation of changing drastically in five minutes. Several times a year, the evening news reports lives lost to avalanches, treacherous falls, and lightning strikes.

In a certain way, life doesn't care either. That is, it knows we will learn valuable lessons whether we fail or succeed at our endeavors. It holds no judgment as to whether we are married for two years or fifty. It doesn't care if we are crying or happy. All of life offers valuable experiences, and all experiences are held in unconditional love.

Part of signing up for this journey includes hurt, disappointment, fear, heartbreak, failure, and betrayal. The worst pain can come from the people who love us most. After all, those are the people we are most vulnerable with. Rather than huddling in a corner clutching our stories, we need to sign up for the whole journey. We need to cultivate compassion for the young ego self inside who suffered those hurts, and for the mature adult who holds the capacity to see it all more clearly. We need to stand in the middle of life, compassion and kindness in hand, prepared to receive whatever weather blows our way.

Self-knowledge gives us choice. Choosing to know ourselves gives us freedom. We can stay unconscious and buy into the latest version of fear's dramatic story, or we can label it, "story, story" and come back into the present. Every moment, we can witness our pain, our hurt, our jealousy, our restlessness directly, and know in our great hearts that it is not all of who we are. Every moment, we can choose to hold whatever weather life brings, in love, compassion, gratitude, and unlimited joy. As one devoted saint put it, "Thank you. I have no complaints whatsoever."

Practice Tools:

1. Have fun recognizing the stories you've grown attached to over the years. Drop all judgment. Be amused by your own personal "oldies but goodies." When you are driving, working, eating, shopping, or making love, notice the "story" playing in your mind. Every time the phone rings, or your watch beeps, let it be a "signal" to tune in to your current story. The second you recognize a story, label it, "story, story" and let it go. Don't let it finish its sentence. Bring yourself back into the present by asking yourself, "Am I here now?"

2. Whenever you "hear" a favorite story playing in your mind, say yes to it and let it go. Practice taking one step back, closing your eyes, taking some deep breaths, and connecting with your Being Self. From this place, "witness" the story from a kind, loving, nonjudgmental—but also nonbelieving—place. Look upon it as you do a fantasy (or a nightmare): interesting, provocative, but not real.

3. Get in the habit of *talking about* your story with your lover, spouse, or friend. That is, rather than believing the story, say, "And now the story is telling me that I shouldn't trust you because you hurt me that one time. And now it's telling me I can't trust anybody." When you relate stories out loud like this, they stop sounding so logical and valid and believable. They sound much more entertaining and amusing but a far cry from the truth.

4. Respond from your Being Self with loving compassion—loving your young ego self for running stories out of habit, simply because it's too scared to feel the raw energy directly. Don't make it bad or judge it harshly. Embrace it with unconditional love. Then love the part of you that is willing to feel all your feelings directly. Make up a new mythology, based on your wise, mature Being Self.

Getting to Know...

Deep Mind Pockets

This joy is what I am, and what you are. It is life
itself, expressing at the highest vibration... It is
at this level of vibration that creation occurs.

—NEALE DONALD WALSCH

I t's in our nature, as human beings, to gravitate toward what is
familiar. When it's snowing or raining in winter, or the smell of
lilacs permeates the air in spring, or hot sun makes our bodies sweat
in summertime, our whole being relaxes with the familiarity and pre-
dictability of such sameness. Right now, as I watch the snow falling
outside my window this morning, I notice my body relaxing; I grew
up in Minnesota and this scene is so familiar, so comforting. We have
our favorite hangouts where we like to meet friends we love, the aroma
of our favorite foods cooking in the kitchen. We even have our favorite
beach or mountaintop for hanging out and reflecting on life.

The same is true with our minds. Our minds have their favorite
pockets they gravitate toward to make sense out of life, especially if
faced with traumatic events or unexpected surprises. These "deep pockets" help us relax, even if they aren't always healthy for us.

The problem is, life isn't predictable. Not really. Our minds, in their
need for safety and security, make it *seem as if* we go to the same workplace with the same people doing the same job every day, but really,
each moment is brand-new. Our bodies, our health, our relationships,
our children, our lives are changing all the time. In fact, as the saying
goes, "the only constant is change." Buddha taught extensively about the
impermanence of life. This reality can be unnerving, especially for our
minds.

To cope with this unpredictability and constant change, we carve
deep, wide, four-lane grooves in our minds—pockets we repeatedly
return to out of habit when something frightens us, or our trust is
broken, or loved ones throw us a wild curve ball. These mind pockets
often get their start in childhood. Like a belief, they are reactions to
traumatic events. If Mom was always crying and Dad was working all
the time, our young self might have concluded, "There's no room for
my feelings," which was true at the time. By the time we're adults, this

habitual way of thinking has already worn a deep groove in our mind.

So every time our mate or good friend is too busy to hear our feelings, the mind dives immediately into the "There's no room for my feelings" pocket without even thinking about it. Deep mind pockets actually prevent us from seeing the present situation clearly, and prevent us from asking clearly for what we need. Our knee-jerk mind pocket says, "Don't even think about it. I'll remind you that there never has been any room for your feelings, and then you'll feel the old, familiar, safe feeling you always have, and you can find comfort in that." For some of us, worry and anxiety compose our habitual mind pocket, and we find ourselves hanging out there often, as if it were our favorite café. Others spend hours and entire relationships hanging out in complaining, or comparing, or not caring in smug indifference. The paths to these favorite hangouts in our minds become so well worn that we routinely stumble into them without realizing it.

But these deep pockets are not our friends, not really. For example, Jake has his own personalized mind pocket that he slips in and out of frequently. When he's in it, he has great trouble seeing it clearly, even though he is a very intelligent man. Over and over, because it's such a deep pocket, it snows him. Last week, he arrived in my office very upset. We had already worked on his old belief—*nobody cares about my needs*—so he knew it had started in childhood with his highly critical parents, but we had already established that it was not true in his current life. However, when he had a major run-in with his son, his "nobody cares" feelers were up on red alert and caught him off-guard.

"You won't believe this," he told me, as if he knew for sure this time that his family didn't care about his needs. "I arrived home Tuesday night, exhausted. I'm out there supporting my family all day, every day, so I figure my son can help me prepare the house for company that's arriving the next day. But when I ask Timothy, my seventeen-year-old, to put sheets on the guest bed for Uncle Harold, he refuses. He says he has plans. He said he'd help later, but I knew better. So once again, I'm doing all the family chores by myself. I swear, nobody does care about my needs—after all I've done for them."

Jake spent the week in a bad mood, shut off from his family. "Everyone knew I was upset," he said. "They all tiptoed around me, but nobody talked about it."

He looked as if he was stuck in a hole the size of the Grand Canyon with no way to get out. But I knew exaggeration would help him shift gears and witness his pattern. "Stand up, Jake. Walk around my office,"

I instructed. "Indulge this brooding character who tells you that nobody cares about you. Say his thoughts out loud. Be his posture."

This was all the permission Jake needed to storm around and brood to his heart's content.

"Who taught you this art of brooding," I asked with an impish grin, "and to brood for days on end?" He furrowed his brow, closed his eyes to think, then answered, "Both of my parents. Mom would never say she was upset, but everyone within a ten-mile radius knew she was. Dad, too, silently sulked in a corner with his books for days." He smiled, signaling that he had just stepped out of his "nobody cares" pocket.

"What I'm curious about," I continued, "is how you, personally, suffered last week, Jake, by buying into your old, familiar mind pocket? What happened to your joy and inner peace when you chose to brood for four days rather than share your feelings?"

"I don't want to keep doing this," he admitted. "I know I alienated my family with anger when my children were growing up. But I was younger then, and less conscious. I don't want to keep misperceiving them, and I don't want them to keep feeling scared of me. I want them to feel loved, and I want to feel their love."

When he went home that night, Jake did something very non-Jake-like. He called a family meeting. He apologized to his wife and children for withdrawing last week, and for all the times he had lost his temper over the years. Then he told his wife he needed help to break this pattern. He said, "When you notice me brooding and withdrawing, please ask me what I'm feeling, because I can't always recognize it when I'm immersed in it." She looked confused at first. But when he explained how desperately he wanted to change his old pattern, she agreed—as long as he promised not to yell at the children. Over some months, with a strong intention and his wife's help, Jake was able to change the pattern.

Notice Your Deep Mind Pockets to Stop Buying into Them

It's easy to see Jake's pattern. It's not as easy to see our own. Our own deep mind pockets feel so natural and normal and real. It's easy to mistake them for "the way life is." We have dropped down into the same old pockets for so many years that we often aren't even looking for a way out. Why would we want to let go of something that has kept us safe all these years, or at least felt as if it did? But when we sincerely ask ourselves, "What price do I pay for my deep pockets in lost joy and peace of mind?" the motivation becomes clear. As we say yes to recognizing our own deep mind pockets, we free ourselves to bask in inner joy. As Pema Chodron said, "If we really knew how unhappy it was making this whole planet that we all try to avoid pain and seek pleasure, then we would practice as if our hair were on fire."

My deep pocket was judgment. I judged myself harshly for years. I judged those close to me more harshly than I care to admit. Sometimes I used my years of meditation and therapy to justify judging everything and everyone harshly. It wasn't until my mid-forties, when chronic digestive pain forced me into it, that I finally asked, "How am I suffering by my own reaction?" With this invitation, my heart opened. I saw how isolated I had made myself for years. I grieved for some time. I stopped seeing judgment as my friend. It still shows up in my awareness (no matter how many times I've tried to send it to the Bahamas for a permanent vacation), but it occupies only minutes of my day, not hours and days. When it comes, I try to remember to respond differently. I let my Being Self feel compassion for the young ego self that still wants to hide behind judgment.

Simply labeling these old, deep mind pockets isn't always enough to counteract the powerful force they have become in our psyches. Sometimes we label them, "worry, worry" or, "fearing, fearing" and they just bounce right back into our minds a minute later, which can make us feel very discouraged. But it's important not to give up.

We just need stronger tools. We need a sharp sword that cuts through these strong habits that paint an illusion of reality and try to make us believe it. We need a strong intention and an eagle's eye to see them clearly for what they are, and persist in letting them go. We build deep inner strength and trust by knowing, in our bones, that it is time to let go — not of their tight grip on us, but of our tight, clingy grasp on them. And for this, we need to grow more and more comfortable with the unpredictable nature of life.

Uncover the Feeling and Belief Fueling Your Mind Pockets

One of my fondest commentaries on human nature came during the Jane Wagner play starring Lily Tomlin, *The Search for Signs of Intelligent Life in the Universe*. Lily pretends to be from another planet, as well as portraying various human characters throughout the play. In one scene, with Post-it notes plastered all over her arms and torso, Lily is pondering the nature of human beings. Suddenly a booming, God-like voice from above asks her, "So why did humans invent the English language anyway?" Lily replies, in so many words, "I'm not exactly sure why. It appears they may have invented it so they could *complain*."

The sad fact is, we spend a lot of our time complaining, worrying, and comparing ourselves to others. All of these—and more—are simply tricks for pulling ourselves out of the present, which inadvertently pulls us out of joy. If we want to feel joy more, it's vital to notice *where we focus our attention*. That is, what do I let my mind chew on? When I speak, what do I waste my breath on? Do I complain about the past, or make a request in present time? Am I comparing myself to others, or basking in the gratitude and grace of this moment? As we witness where we are placing our attention, we free ourselves to choose joy.

Deep mind pockets will steal our joy until we let go of our tight grip on them.

Many of us these days are living our dream. We are living with the person we fell madly in love with months or years ago. We are doing the work we chose, or we are taking actions to build our dream career. We are raising the children we chose to have and whom we love more than life. And yet, in the day-to-day-ness of daily life, when boredom strikes, or mud is tracked through the house, we easily forget we are living our dream.

I invite you to carve out new mind pockets for yourself—ones labeled gratitude, forgiveness, compassion, and humor. Even in this moment, choose joy. No matter what complaint is tugging at your attention, witness it with amusement. Let your huge Being Self hold all of your old, familiar, well-worn mind pockets in loving compassion. Gently remind yourself, "I'm living the life I created, even if I'm upset in this moment."

See how you are steeped in grace, even now. Appreciate this precious life.

Practice Tools:

1. Name one deep pocket your mind tends to return to repeatedly. Invite it into your awareness without any judgment. Practice saying yes to it and letting it go. Stop buying into its story and letting it convince you that fear is right. Witness your deep mind pocket from a neutral, compassionate place.
2. Whether your most common mind pockets fall under the category of judgment, doubt, fear, worry, complaining, or comparing, set an

intention to recognize your deep mind pockets whenever they come up. Every morning, say, "I'm willing to notice whenever this deep mind pocket arises and tries to steal my joy." Exaggerate it for two minutes in a private room to help you consciously recognize it.

3. Identify the unexpressed feeling that lives underneath your deepest mind pocket. Set aside thirty minutes. Find a quiet, private room where you can lie down, close your eyes, take some deep breaths, and ask yourself, "What feeling lives underneath this deep mind pocket?" Just breathe deeply and listen for the answer. When you identify the feeling, ask, "Where does this feeling live in my body?" Take deep breaths, breathing directly down into the feeling until it fully releases. Then focus around your heart and softly ask your inner wisdom, "How can I be free of this mind pocket completely? What do I need to let go of to return to inner joy?"

Belief Habits

*This is your body, your greatest gift, pregnant
with wisdom you do not hear, grief you thought
was forgotten, and joy you have never known.*
—MARION WOODMAN

CORE BELIEFS LIE DEEP IN THE BASEMENT OF OUR UNCONSCIOUS, fueling unexpressed feelings. Unexpressed feelings fuel obsessive thoughts, worries, plans, and regrets. In healing, we reverse the direction. We use obsessive thoughts to help us identify which core belief is fueling our unexpressed feelings. Then we face and express the feelings directly. This dismantling is easier if we are willing to identify our underlying beliefs.

It can feel challenging at first to name our core beliefs and make them conscious. Such beliefs as, "I'm unworthy," "I don't deserve love," or, "nobody cares about my needs" join our lives so early in life. As infants and young children, during a traumatic event, we welcome one of these core beliefs into our psyche to help make sense of an adult world that is too overwhelming at the time. Over the years, they no longer sound like beliefs at all. They sound like truth, reality, the way life is. They feel solid, like cement. They filter our perceptions. If we let them, they block us from reaching out into the world to get our needs met. They stop us from remembering that, on a Being level, we always deserve to feel heard, seen, and acknowledged, no matter what is happening.

The good news is, we can change old beliefs in a few moments. The second we name our core belief, we can create a new belief to match the truth of our Being now. "I'm unworthy" becomes, "I'm completely worthy and deserving of love." Ultimately, as we reclaim our power, hold old core beliefs in love, and embrace new beliefs that match who we are now, we expand into joyful cocreators of the Universe.

"I Can't Have What I Want Here"

Great fullness of being, which we experience
as happiness, can also be described
as love. To be undivided and unfragmented,
to be completely present, is to love.

—SHARON SALZBERG

D ave was referred by his doctor for depression. In many people's eyes, Dave had it made. He retired in his early fifties, living off interest from his investments and property holdings. Ten years ago he had left New York City to live "in the mountains" in Colorado. But he felt lonely, isolated, depressed. He became discouraged while coping with age-related health issues. He said, "I can't find my soul mate here, and I don't feel a sense of community here. I guess I have to move back to the Big Apple."

Rather than buying into his unconscious belief—*I can't get what I want here*—and getting lost in the elaborate story he had devised with it, I cut to the chase. I asked Dave, "So how long have you been buying into this belief?"

"What belief?" he retorted, sounding annoyed.

"The belief that you can't get what you want where you are," I replied.

He looked sheepish, as if his hand had been caught in the cookie jar. He jumped into his usual first line of defense, as we all do. "I've tried, Carolyn. I really have. I dated this woman friend for six months, but we turned out to be just good friends. No romance. I've gone out on blind dates that friends set me up with. But you know, I had a painful first marriage, and I just don't think . . ." He began running his life story of failed relationships, but I stopped him.

"Wait a second," I interrupted. "Instead of talking about it, would you be willing to exaggerate this belief with your whole body for two minutes?" I knew something Dave didn't know, that exaggeration is a fun way to bring beliefs out of the closet to be seen.

He agreed, but he looked stiff and self-conscious. I prodded him. "Teach me what you know about this belief. How does it talk to you? Does it yell at you? Shame you? Guilt-trip you? Does it sound like the fatherly voice of reason? How does it convince you to give up what you want so easily?" I encouraged. "Walk around the room and show me how this character inside you moves through the world. Say its thoughts out loud."

Old Beliefs Prove Themselves Right at Our Expense

Dave reluctantly agreed. He slumped forward, rounded his shoulders, and lumbered around my office. His head hung down. "You'll never find what you want here," he said in a monotone voice. "This town's too small. All the good women are taken, or they're already your friends. Go back to the city, where you belong. Besides, marriage was hell— why risk another broken heart?"

When he spoke these last words, he looked as if a light bulb had lit up inside. Tears filled his eyes. For the first time, he let himself fully grieve over how lonely he had felt for the eighteen years of his first marriage. Then, in a tender voice, he told me how scared he was to receive the kind of love he'd never had from his parents or his wife. "I believe that kind of love is possible," he said. "I've seen friends who have it. I just don't know if I get to have it in this lifetime."

Unconscious beliefs fuel our unexpressed feelings—feelings we have often been too scared to feel for years. Once Dave touched down into his grief and fear, he no longer needed to buy into this sabotaging belief. I asked him to stand and face me, making eye contact with me, and say what he wanted his new belief to sound like. "I'd like to find the love and sense of belonging I want right here. But I just don't know if I ever will, and I can't keep wasting time . . ."

I gently interrupted. "Let's leave the 'buts' out for now—that's just fear trying to prevent you from risking. Say how you would like it to be if you knew for sure that the Universe wants to give you what you want. Start with 'I'm willing to . . .'"

He thought for a moment. Then he took a deep breath, looked straight into my eyes, and said, "I'm willing to receive the caring love and community I so long for right here." A wide, ten-year-old grin came across his face at the possibility. I said, "Great. Now, say your belief one more time, but as if it's already true."

He said, "I have the caring love and sense of community I want right here where I live." He promised to repeat his new belief to himself every morning for a month.

Six months later, Dave came to see me. He had decided to create his own community by buying "a beautiful piece of ranch land," in his words. He was in the process of inviting local schools and groups to participate in community projects on the land and receiving a great response. "But as I get closer to manifesting my dream," he said, "my old belief is rearing its ugly head. I need your help." Together, we explored the origin of this old belief—a deep fear of never feeling loved by his father. By making this conscious, and loving it, he reconnected with his inner joy. A year later, I saw Dave at a restaurant. He introduced me to the woman sitting beside him. "We've been seeing each other for six months," he beamed. Once he embraced his new belief, and expressed the grief and fear fueling his old belief, Dave moved full speed ahead.

Old beliefs are like clouds, covering up our inner joy and love. We trust that clouds will move on and reveal the sun, but we tend to forget that our inner joy and love will return as soon as the old belief disappears. These old beliefs sabotage our joy and our dreams, without our even knowing it. They hang around for so many years, sounding so logical and practical, they become our truth. When we cling to the belief that we can't get what we want in this relationship, in this town, in this lifetime, we prove it right. We block ourselves from receiving the joy and love that is always present.

The best love we have ever known could be standing right in front of us, but we can't feel it, we can't see it, we can't let it in. Our belief won't let us. Beliefs sound so real because we've held onto them for so long. When we were tiny infants or small children experiencing trauma, our minds offered us some fear-based belief to appease us. At the time, with no way to comprehend the bigger picture, we clung to it for safety. We lacked the ability to do otherwise. We were too overwhelmed by this complex world to discriminate between the voice of fear and the voice of love. We held on tight, grateful for the life jacket. And we've been holding on ever since, doing whatever it took to prove the old beliefs right.

The good news is that we can create new, healthy beliefs to replace those old, limiting ones—and we can do it in about five minutes. You read that right. Five minutes. Contrary to the myth perpetuated by some people in psychology, you don't have to spend years analyzing your childhood to change your outlook. You just need to bring the belief fully into your conscious awareness, witness it, name it, and respond differently. *Now* is always the best time to reexamine our beliefs, because all the power is in the present.

Witnessing Old Beliefs Frees Us to Respond Differently

Since many of our deep-set beliefs tend to take hold during a childhood trauma (when we had to sacrifice the integrity of our Being for love, food, and shelter), it can be difficult to see them at first. This is true even with the best intentions. But once we stand back and witness an old belief, we free ourselves to choose a healthier response.

For example, Suzie's stepfather molested her. When she finally told her mother, her mother refused to believe her. Instead, she blamed Suzie. Suzie felt she had no alternative but to hide her shame by escaping into books and scholastic achievements. To make sense out of a crazy-making situation, she started to believe: "My needs must not be important. Nobody cares about me because something is wrong with me."

Now, forty years later, in a loving relationship, Suzie has a great deal of trouble expressing her needs to her husband. Her old belief runs her show so thoroughly that it has convinced her that she doesn't have needs. When a strong need manages to get her attention, she doesn't feel safe enough to express it.

By the time she arrived in my office, her old belief had convinced her that she couldn't trust her husband with her needs. She acted this out by pushing him away. After fully expressing her rage, grief, and fear around being molested, she was able to name her old belief and stop buying into it. She instantly created a new, healthy belief: "My needs are important. I care about my needs, and I teach my husband how to care about my needs." She practices recognizing her needs, and voicing them, every day.

Fear-based beliefs can also become locked into place during adult traumas. Joan suffered severe anxiety and panic attacks following a car accident. As with most post-traumatic-stress victims, she felt extremely vulnerable every waking moment. Life suddenly looked like a series of endless possibilities for getting hurt, or even killed. Her all-consuming belief following this trauma was, "I'm not safe." She stopped driving. She stopped going out at night. She even stopped wanting a child, since that child could get hurt. She felt a level of anxiety she had never experienced before. In her fearful mind, every street corner looked like an accident waiting to happen.

The first thing I did was help her to identify her old belief. Once she was able to name it, her identity began to shift and expand. She was able to see the old belief for exactly what it was—a fear-based belief—and reassure her young ego self that, in this moment, she was safe. She also closed her eyes, located the fear in her body, and focused directly on it. After she had faced her fear directly, her eyes and face looked much more relaxed.

I asked her, "Now, what would you like your new belief to be, Joan?"

"That I'm safe," she replied. "The accident reminded me what vulnerable human beings we all are. But on a deep, mature Being level, I know that I am safe."

I saw her five years later on the street, holding her baby boy in her arms. "Look, Carolyn, my son Jason," she grinned. "I've been meaning to tell you for a long time, that accident was one of the best things that happened to me. Now I'm married, and this is my second child. I was blinded by my own fears long before that accident woke me up."

It's not what happens to us that matters so much as how we respond. We live in these vulnerable human bodies. We can expect hurt and disappointment, even trauma at times, as part of the human experience. What matters is identifying the beliefs that solidify in our minds around what happens to us. It matters a great deal to us, and to our ongoing experience of inner joy. Here are some simple exercises to create healthy new beliefs.

Practice Tools:

1. Pick an issue that keeps showing up in your life, one that's frustrating you lately. Close your eyes and take some deep breaths in your belly. Then ask yourself, "What old, familiar belief is fueling this pattern?" It could be one you thought you got over years ago, such as, "I'm not good enough." Or it could be a belief you've clung to for so many years, you forgot it was a belief at all, such as, "There is no space for my needs" or, "I'm not important." Just ask inside, take several deep breaths, and listen for whatever words or feelings bubble up. Your inner wisdom is lounging around inside, just waiting for you to call on it. Ask away!

2. Now that you have identified and named your old, unconscious belief, let it go. Write the belief down on a piece of paper, read it out loud, and burn it as a symbolic ritual to let go of an especially tough belief. Then close your eyes and ask yourself, "What would I like my new belief to sound like?" Repeat your new belief to yourself every morning until it becomes part of you.

3. What would you ask if you knew you were completely safe to be exactly who you are at a deep soul level? Ask, "What would my Inner Self like to hear?" Beliefs should be one simple sentence, easy to remember, such as, "I am lovable," "Who I am is well received," or,

"I have plenty of space to feel and express my needs." Once you've named your new belief, write it down. Each morning, and through the day, say your new belief under your breath, especially when you notice fear or doubt telling you otherwise. Creating a new belief changes how you ask for what you want, and how you teach others to respect you and your needs. Say your new belief, and watch how your response to life changes.

"Nobody Cares about My Needs"

It's so simple to live. So simple to be happy, so
simple to be always in bliss . . . Allow some time,
just a moment, to see who you are.
—H. W. L. POONJA

L ike iris and tulip bulbs in winter, beliefs can lie dormant deep in our
unconscious for years, running our lives and our relationships.
And because they are buried out of sight, they can do all this without
our realizing it. Such is the case with the prevalent but often unacknowledged belief, "Nobody cares about my needs."

In my therapy with couples, one or both people in the relationship
often express this belief. Of course, they don't communicate it consciously. Few of us know how to say, "My 'nobody cares' belief is up
again, hon, so I need time for you to listen to my needs." Instead, we are
completely immersed in it, buying into it, believing every word. "If
you really loved me," we blurt out angrily, "you'd know what I need
and stop making me always have to ask for it." But even more frequently,
we gave up asking long ago and decided that our mate just isn't capable of responding to our needs.

We Have to Honor Our Own Needs First

We often *don't know how* to create space for our needs. We never learned.
We all have basic human needs for touch, connection, feeling heard
and seen, and sexual contact. Beyond that, few of us have learned to
respond to our needs from our wise Being Self. When we were growing up, we were taught that our higher needs—to be heard, acknowledged, and honored from our soul level—didn't matter. Our parents
did what they believed by focusing on our physical needs. They provided
food, shelter, and clothing. They spanked or yelled or sent us to our
rooms because that's what they believed was right. Parents didn't understand the inner needs of our highly sensitive Being Selves because they
had never learned about their own sensitive Being Selves.

Therefore, it's up to us to bring this to ourselves. It's up to us to see,
hear, honor, and acknowledge these higher needs.

Jungian analyst Marion Woodman writes in *Coming Home to Myself,*

"Deep rage is this: Nobody ever saw me. Nobody ever heard me. As long as I can remember, I've had to perform. When I tried to be myself, I was told, 'That's not what you think, that's not what you ought to do.' . . . That's deep rage."

If we go unconscious, this deep rage gets unleashed on our spouse or lover. We all walk through the world desperate to have *someone, somewhere* really see us, hear us, and acknowledge us at this deep soul level. But whatever comes from the outside will never be enough. We must see and hear our own Inner Selves. And that takes developing a healthy relationship with our Being Self, which means spending some time each day getting to know ourselves at the soul level.

Whether you spend one hour, two hours, or thirty minutes, won't matter that much in the end. The important thing is that you step into the open space set aside and ask, "What sounds good right now?" Don't plan it ahead of time. Let your body and soul discover what it needs in the present. See if it wants to dance to music, paint, sing, draw, or roller blade. And the amount of time may vary from day to day, depending on what else is on your plate. However long you give yourself is fine. Just do it. Just start. If you have no time today, block out an hour tomorrow, or two hours Saturday morning. Begin now making a date with your soul. Write it in your datebook like any other appointment.

Blaming Loved Ones Is Often Our First Clue to Our Pattern

How often do you catch yourself mumbling, "Nobody cares about *my* needs. Everybody else's needs are so important, they need it *right now*, like it's life or death. But nobody's listening to me. Nobody asks me. What I need doesn't matter, not enough."

Pretty soon, we not only stop voicing our needs, we forget that we have any.

But it's when we *stop* voicing our needs that our relationships get into trouble. Resentment builds. Communication breaks down. Which is what happened for Stan.

Stan and Carol came to me to save their marriage. Actually Stan wanted a separation, and Carol wanted them to stay together. The underlying issue took some time to uncover. Their sex life was non-existent. "I was frigid," Carol admitted, "because I had been molested. But I worked through that in therapy. Then Stan quit initiating."

"Stan, would you be willing to talk about *your* part?" I prodded.

He pressed his lips together and glanced at Carol. "I don't know," he shrugged. "I heard how horrible being molested was for her. And

I've heard stories from other women about molestation. I just didn't want to be one more man pushing my sexual needs on her."

Carol was weeping. "Oh, Stan, you've always been such a sweet, sensitive man. That's why I married you. When I was working on being molested in therapy, I had to tell you about it so you knew what I went through, and so I could heal. But I never intended for us to stop having sex." They both agreed to talk about their sexual needs much more with each other. Stan worked on his habit of postponing his needs.

Creating a Safe, Sacred Space to Voice Our Needs

Once we've spent some time listening to our needs, the next step is to express them. For some people this can feel terrifying, especially around their most tender, vulnerable needs. It helps a great deal to create a sacred space within which to communicate our needs clearly. This was an important step for Peggy.

Peggy had worked hard on herself in individual therapy. Enough so that she planned to leave her boyfriend because he was such a poor listener. When she finally told him about leaving, he begged her to try couple's therapy first. She agreed, reluctantly.

During their first session, she sat defiantly with her arms crossed. "You never listen to my needs!" she snarled. "You're always too busy, too tired, too something. You can't only tell me you love me when you want sex. You have to *show me* you love me. And frankly, you failed miserably. That's why I'm leaving."

Charlie was begging her to stay, but I interrupted him. "Peggy," I asked, "would you be willing to tell Charlie what you need in the relationship? Would you be willing to teach him what phrases he might use to encourage you to keep sharing your feelings? Which gestures helped you feel heard in the past?" Her jaw hung open in disbelief.

"Are you telling me it's my fault?" she accused me.

"No, not at all," I replied. "I actually don't believe in fault. I believe in the truth, and I believe in solutions. The best solution I know, once you know what your needs are, is to create an uninterrupted, sacred space for communicating them. Make sure you're heard. Are you willing to try that?"

"What's a sacred space?" she sneered, rolling her eyes.

"Creating a sacred space means carving out special time, away from the phone and children, for the two of you to listen to each other's needs, uninterrupted. You have been sabotaging your own needs by failing to communicate them clearly, or throwing them out during inappropriate times, such as when Charlie is headed out the door for work. In this moment, I invite you to teach Charlie how you'd like him to treat your needs. Turn your complaints into a request."

She slowly nodded, as if it was starting to make sense, barely. "Go ahead," I said, "tell Charlie what you need. Be as specific and clear as possible. Expect him to listen to you. Demand it. Pretend you are stuck loving Charlie for the rest of your life, with no escape hatch, and you really need him to pay attention to you and to hear your needs."

I shifted to look at Charlie. "Now Charlie, I invite *you* to listen intently because you will be telling Peggy exactly what you heard her say when she's done."

"What the hell," Peggy shrugged, "I've got nothing more to lose at this point. Charlie, when I say I need to share feelings, I need you to look me in the eye and *really* listen. Put down your newspaper, stop watching TV, and listen like you care. I need to feel like you *care* about my needs and feelings. I need you to *acknowledge* what you heard me say before you jump in with your opinion. That's what makes me feel loved."

They went home to practice. Gradually, over time, their conflicts diminished. Peggy became good at creating a sacred space for sharing her needs. After working with them for three months, Peggy was excited to share her news. "We're getting married."

Many of us gave up on getting our deepest needs met long ago. We walled off our needs, and our pain of not getting them met, in defense. Men, for instance, might not have trouble vocalizing their sexual needs, but they rarely know where to begin sharing their need for touch, cuddling, or being held when they need to cry. Women, on the other hand, tend to give up too easily, concluding that there is no room for their needs, before they have really tried. Meanwhile, our Being Self waits patiently for us to hear and see ourselves.

In fact, we were taught that part of being "grown up" meant sacrificing our own needs and feelings to serve others. Let's replace that belief with the idea that there is plenty of room to honor others' needs and take time to listen to and honor our own needs, including our soul's needs. Once this skill is honed, mature adults teach loved ones, including their children, how to listen to and honor their needs. This is the new, responsible, mature, wise Being that we are striving to connect with. This is responding differently, to ourselves and others, from our Being Self with an open, compassionate heart. This is reclaiming our joy, pure and simple.

Practice Tools:

1. If you have a tendency to blame others for not caring about your needs, take responsibility for abandoning your own needs. Say yes to the old habit without judgment. "Yes, I have been blaming others." Then ask yourself, "How am I not listening to my needs?" See if you can name your belief, whether it's, "Nobody cares about my needs" or, "There's never time for my needs."

2. Set a few minutes aside each day to lie down, close your eyes, and ask your Inner Self, "What do I need?" Take some deep breaths in your belly, and patiently wait for a phrase, feeling sense, or picture to bubble up into your awareness. Try saying every morning, "I listen to, acknowledge, and honor my needs. And I make time to teach others how to listen to and honor my needs."

3. Take out a sheet of paper or a journal. Witness your needs by finishing this sentence over and over: "If I were listening to me, I would _____." Write down every crazy and not-so-crazy longing that pops into your head. Don't plan it. Just write what comes. You can vary it at other times by starting with, "If I were listening to my soul _____." or "If I were listening to my Inner Self _____." When I was ill from exhaustion one time, this exercise helped shine a light on what my body and soul needed to come back into balance.

4. Practice creating a sacred space for sharing your feelings. Tell your spouse, lover, or loved one, "I have some needs to share with you. When would be a good time for you to listen to me? I need about _____ minutes of uninterrupted time, though if it turns into deeper feelings than I first anticipated, I'd like you to be open to giving it more time." State your needs clearly and specifically. Teach the other person whether being held, or feeling heard without interruption, or hearing reassuring words helps you the most to share vulnerable needs. Practice this each week with a loved one until this becomes your new habit. It can also be done lying in bed, or in front of the fireplace, facing each other, touching and looking into each other's eyes. Affection, appreciation, and acknowledgment go a long way in creating intimacy, in relating to ourselves and loved ones.

"I'm Not Good Enough"

Do you hear? If you do, you hear the heart
speaking to itself purely and simply... If there is
something at stake,... you will be too busy
attending to that fear or belief to hear.

—GANGAJI

Enlightenment through boredom. That is what my spiritual teacher and psychic friend, Teresa, calls it when the same beliefs recycle back through our lives again and again, until we finally learn what our souls have been trying to teach us. The "not good enough" belief is one that can take a lifetime to dismantle, unless we face it straight on. Remember Al Franken's Stuart Smalley character on *Saturday Night Live*, saying, "I'm good enough! I'm smart enough! And, gosh darn it, people like me." We laughed because part of us identified with that rather pathetic little guy needing affirmation.

Unfortunately, laughing won't make it go away. Nor will thinking. The "not good enough" saboteur is wily and sneaky, like a coyote. As soon as we get a grip in one area of our lives, it attacks another. We feel "good enough" in our work and it attacks our weight, or our parenting skills, our disappearing sex appeal, or our ineptness in handling our aging parents. It steals our joy no matter how hard we pretend it's not there.

There's Maggie, who had several affairs over a five-year stretch before she finally declared herself important enough to leave her husband. There's John, whose yardstick always measured "not good enough," even though he cared for his aging mother before and after work seven days a week, until finally his body gave out. He was sick for six weeks, which shook him up enough to place her in a good nursing home.

There's Roxie, whose success was never good enough for her mother, even though by her mid-thirties her annual income was twice that of her husband. There's Joyce, who tried to get over her husband's seven-year affair all by herself because her "not good enough" voice kept her from asking him to come to therapy. There's Martha, who is excellent at teaching first and second graders, but balks at the principal's rave evaluations each year. In her eyes, she's still not good enough. Otherwise, why would those five neighbor boys have molested her when she was six years old?

I could go on and on. No matter how successful we look on the outside, too often we secretly struggle with "not good enough" voices inside. It's like an epidemic.

Most of us keep a secret tally sheet tucked inside our minds. And when we feel down, lonely, or scared, we pull it out to review the score: "I'm not good enough because my business failed. I'm divorced. I'm not a good enough parent. I had an abortion. I had sex, lots of it, out of wedlock. I made love to a woman, and I am a woman. Or I fell in love with a man, a married man. I'm a recovering addict. My wife left me." Guilt, shame, judgment, and doubt all pile on top of each other, deeming us not good enough.

Women feel pressured to be company CEO *and* outstanding mother of the year, inevitably falling into the "not good enough" hole on both counts, or having heart attacks trying. Men feel pressure to provide unlimited abundance for their families *and* reopen their sensitive feeling side (which usually gets slammed shut in boys by about first grade). No matter how well they do on either count, it's never enough. It's as if, deep inside, we all fear that our gravestone will say in bold, black letters, "Good provider, lover, spouse, parent, environmentalist, neighbor, and friend, **but not good enough**."

I'm no exception. This fall, my "not good enough" monster pounced on the reality that my mother was dying. When she was given two to four months to live, I freaked out. Part of me wanted to sit by her bedside and hold her hand every minute until she took her last breath. But I had a therapy practice and a book manuscript due in six months. When I called my psychic friend, Teresa, who has known me for twenty years, she was concerned. "I know you've worked through this 'not good enough' on many levels," she said, "but it's enlightenment through boredom again. However you love your mother in these final months, keep reminding yourself that it's good enough."

The "not good enough" voice may grow quieter and subtler inside. It may shift topics. If we catch it right away, it may last only two minutes instead of two hours, or two days. But the truth is, it doesn't go away. It comes and goes as it pleases, triggered by any number of things that are completely out of our control. What we can do is say yes to it when it comes and keep telling ourselves, "Whatever I'm doing, it's good enough."

Inviting "Not Good Enough" in for a Cup of Tea

Our best defense against "not good enough" is a simple aikido move: to welcome it graciously into our awareness and send it right back out again, all in one smooth move. Invite it in for a cup of tea, but not a two-hour dinner. Say yes to it. Be curious about it. Wonder, "How might 'not good enough' be showing up in my life now?" (even if you believe it's long gone). Practice witnessing it from your mature Being Self. Give it as much credibility as you might give an Alzheimer's patient in the final stages. Just stop buying into it.

Sometimes we inherit a "not good enough" belief from a parent or grandparent. It can lie dormant in our cells for years, far below our awareness. Like a rattlesnake hiding in the tall, untamed grass, it can bite us and hurt our life, when we're least expecting it.

Our minds come up with all sorts of reasons to make us feel not good enough. We love to blame something or someone *out there*. But it's rarely anything *out there* making us not good enough. Not really. It's us, projecting our "not good enough" belief onto others, then believing it. Every moment, we choose: to stay unconscious, or see our part in creating it. Every moment, we can reassure ourselves, "What I'm doing, and how I'm doing it, is good enough" or we can slide back down that old, non-risk-taking path.

For some, turning this belief around can feel like hard work. It was for Susan. Her mother was an abusive alcoholic. She never met her father, who died before he turned forty. Her mother found fault with Susan constantly. By seven or eight, she stopped talking, except to say what her mother wanted to hear. When I asked Susan about her needs, she said, "Needs? You didn't have needs around my mother. Needs didn't exist."

Susan grew up believing she really wasn't good enough, not good enough to be loved. How could she conclude anything else from living with a mother who did nothing but judge her daily? When she was molested, she told nobody. "Who was there to tell?" she asked. "My mother would have made it my fault; she made everything my fault."

Every week in therapy, Susan worked hard to reclaim her inner joy. She practiced loving every feeling she used to fear, including disappointment, resentment, and deep grief. In between sessions, she wrestled week after week with the doubt and self-judgment that seemed engraved on her psyche. She practiced meditation. She called old friends and shared her hurt feelings, even though sharing any feelings was scary for her.

She caught herself falling for a lover who was not available emotionally, just as she had done for the past twenty years. But this time, she quickly let it go. Deep in her soul, she began to feel a twinge that maybe, just maybe, she was good enough, even if her mother hadn't been capable of showing it. The more she loved her fear and anxiety and judgment, the more she changed. By Christmastime, she received so many invitations from friends that she spent every minute fitting everybody in. That's why I was so deeply touched on Christmas Day when Susan left this message on my machine: "I got what I wanted for Christmas, Carolyn. I have self-love."

We can't change our past conditioning, or how traumatic our childhoods may have been. But we can respond differently. We can say yes to what is, witness our "not good enough," and respond to *every* feeling from our Being Self, and with compassion.

Practice Tools:

1. Be open to noticing any "not good enough" still lurking in your unconscious, limiting your choices. Listen for whatever needs, longings, and dreams have been silenced out of recognition by this culprit. Ask what risks you might not be taking, what dreams you have postponed because of this trickster. Be curious: "I wonder where that old family heirloom, 'not good enough,' is showing up in my life?" Witness where it stops you from fully expressing yourself.

2. Every hour, every day, for a whole month, tell yourself, "I am good enough." Breathe "I am" in and "good enough" out for ten long breaths. Whisper it to your Inner Self on the subway. Yell it at the top of your lungs in your car. At night in bed, place one hand over your heart and one hand over your belly, and repeat it softly to your Inner Self as you fall asleep.

3. At the top of a piece of paper, write, "Since I'm now good enough, I can . . ." Keep finishing that sentence fifty times. Watch your creative imagination blast wide open. Dust off those old dreams. Let it rip.

Letting Go of the Belief...
"I Have to Blame Myself or Others"

Ultimately, there is no way to escape
taking responsibility for ourselves.
—TARTHANG TULKU

S heila and Dave walked into my office in a loud silence. Dave sat with his arms across his chest, gazing out the window, showing that he didn't really want to be there. Sheila glared, so wide-eyed it looked as if her eyes might explode at any second. "He had an affair!" she blurted out. "I gave him two beautiful children. I supported him through medical school. I've done nothing but stand by his side for fifteen years, and this is how he repays me. What am I supposed to do with that? How can we go on?"

They each spent fifteen minutes telling me "their side" of the story. Then I said, "Let's try something new. You've gone round and round at home with who is right and wrong, and whose fault it is. So let's start by throwing whose fault it is out the window. While we're at it, let's throw right and wrong out the window, too."

Sheila furrowed her brow and glared. "But *he* had the affair!" Sheila persisted. "It's my heart that's torn open and bleeding. I'm not letting him off the hook that easy!"

"Yes, he acted out the pain in your marriage by having an affair, which is an extremely painful breach of trust," I affirmed. "But if you would be willing, Sheila, I'd like to offer your marriage the deepest healing possible. I would like to look at what happened, and the pain on both sides, through a wider lens. As an experiment, I invite both of you to take full responsibility for the affair, and the actions leading up to the affair. Dave, that means you taking 100 percent responsibility for *choosing* to act out your pain by having an affair, and to do so without blaming Sheila in any way. Sheila, I want you to take 100 percent responsibility by looking at *your part* in creating the affair. I ask you to peek underneath your indignation, which you have every right to feel, and see any ways you maybe withdrew your love, or shut down your feelings, or pushed Dave away.

"Compared to how we watched our parents and other adults do relationship," I continued, "this is graduate-level work. So be patient with yourselves. Let your hurt selves take a little time to wrap around this concept. I'm asking for a leap of faith. But frankly, if the right/wrong or blaming each other had worked, you wouldn't be here. So would you be willing, as an experiment?" They both shrugged, then nodded in agreement.

I let out a loud sigh. "Ahhhh, now we have some breathing room. I invite you to take some deep breaths, as if you're flushing out all the old stories and approaching this brand new." They both sighed. "Now I invite you to close your eyes and take several more deep breaths. Drop below the story line and *feel* how the pain of the affair feels in your body. No matter which side of it you stand on, notice where you feel the pain in your body. Notice what feelings it triggers, and how you've reacted to those feelings so far. Just notice with curiosity. Focus directly on the pain, and really feel it."

They both touched some sadness as they did this. "Now, shift awareness to your heart. Imagine breathing in and out of your heart for a few moments. Ask your heart, 'How have I reacted to my pain so far?' Just ask, take a deep breath, let your mind be a blank slate, and see what bubbles up. Once you see your reaction clearly, ask your heart, 'How have I suffered by my reaction?'" Sheila wiped her eyes. Dave shifted in his chair. "Now ask your heart, 'What lesson is here for me to learn if I'm willing to receive it?'"

When they opened their eyes and looked at each other, they both looked softer, less guarded. The energetic shift in the room was palpable. Sheila's indignation melted into raw, tender hurt. Dave uncrossed his arms and reached out to hold Sheila's hands. "I'm so, so sorry," he said. "You pulled away from me a year ago, after your mother passed away, and I couldn't reach you. Whatever I did was wrong. Whatever I tried was rejected. I can't stand how much I hurt you, and I know I can't take it back. I should have talked to you about my pain, but I've always been lousy at sharing my feelings."

Sheila cried. "I'm sorry, too," she confessed. "I knew I was pushing you away, but I couldn't stop myself. When you hugged me, my arms fell limp. When you invited me out to dinner, I refused, thinking you should have done it years ago. I was crazy with grief after Mom died, and I projected my pain onto you. I decided you weren't there for me, you wouldn't listen to my feelings because you never have, and I never gave you a chance. I shut you out. It was the affair that made me realize how much I love you."

After crying for several minutes in silence, she looked at Dave and said, "Deep inside, Dave, I've always been terrified that you might leave me. I've never actually felt worthy of your love. Now, in a way, my worst fear has come true. I, too, should have talked to you about my feelings. Instead, I pushed you right towards her."

They both made a strong commitment to talk about any hurt feelings regularly, each week.

Several month later, after practicing their new skills (and falling back into old habits), they came again for a couple's session. Each day after work, they had gotten in the habit of lying together on the bed, looking into each other's eyes, touching and sharing feelings. Sheila struggled with trusting him with her vulnerable feelings, but as she shared the fears and broken trust that rattled her every day, Dave began to grasp the depth of pain she was experiencing. Dave went back and forth, withdrawing and isolating as he used to, then finding the courage to talk about his feelings. Gradually, he cried in front of her as he talked about the pain of being rejected, and how rejection was a lifetime fear of his. Toward the end of our couple's session, Sheila said, "I never thought I'd say this, but as painful as it was, the affair woke us both up, and brought us together."

Stretching Our Logical Minds to Embrace Responsibility

I remember the first time I heard this strange concept: "Taking 100 percent responsibility." It doesn't add up, mathematically. It was January 1992. I was in Sausalito, California, taking a week-long training in body-centered therapy from Gay and Kathlyn Hendricks. It ruffled my feathers when I first heard it because it didn't make logical sense. Kathlyn taught how each person in a relationship fights for the biggest victim position. Then she had us pair off and act out how we play victim in our lives.

I stood defiantly with my arms crossed. "I don't," I told my workshop partner. "It's not my fault my mate was depressed for two years and refused to work. I felt forced to withdraw. Now, I just can't get past my resentment. I can't forgive and let it go."

Kathlyn was walking by and overheard our discussion. "So act out your resentment, Carolyn," she nudged. "Buying into resentment *is* your victim role. It's your attempt to try to control life by living in the past." Once I exaggerated my resentment, and witnessed it from my Being Self, I saw that it was such a tiny part of who I am. Yet it was consuming most of my waking awareness and dominating my choices. By the end of the week, I jumped at every chance to take 100 percent responsibility for everything: my work, my love life, my unfulfilled dreams. And I've shared this gift with clients every chance I have. Why? Because responsibility spells Freedom, with a capital F. Tremendous freedom. It's the shortcut to inner joy.

Our First Step in Responsibility Is to Know Ourselves

Whether we accept it or not, whether our logical mind is able to wrap around it or spits it out, we are ultimately responsible for how our life is going. Whether we believe it now, or later, we are 100 percent responsible to ourselves for our needs, our feelings, and our heartfelt longings. Blaming, guilt-tripping, shaming, and complaining about who did what to us when is a nasty habit. An unconscious habit we inherited from our ancestors (some of whom apparently had these skills polished to an art form). But when all the blaming, shaming, and complaining is laid to rest, and when we find the courage to toss fault-finding out the window, we are left with our own reactions, habits, and patterns. In that moment, we discover that *we always have a choice* how to respond to whatever sits in front of us. In this discovery of choice, and in coming to know our reactions more fully, we uncover an incredible spaciousness.

As we know ourselves better, we get to ask our wise, tender hearts, "What *feeling* is fueling this story? What *belief* is fueling this unexpressed feeling? What does my Inner Self need or want that, due to past conditioning, I'm scared to ask for?"

If we feel angry, we need to take a few moments to pause and get to know anger in a new way. To notice what anger feels like in our bodies. To notice what beliefs fuel the anger, and what thoughts anger triggers. This is *responding to* anger without acting it out. This empowers us to *talk about* our anger in a way that doesn't push others away.

If loneliness is triggered inside, we can pause for two minutes, close our eyes, and witness how loneliness feels in our bodies. This step interrupts our usual habit of being consumed or lost in loneliness, allowing our essential Being to respond to loneliness with compassion. We can ask, "Given that my lonely button is triggered, what do I need?"

This frees us to respond to our need in this present moment, where all the power is. We can call a friend, journal our feelings, be with the feelings—whatever our soft, quiet Inner Self tells us it needs. This is being response-able to our needs and feelings. Not habitually reacting to our story while abandoning our Inner Self one more time.

Teaching Our Needs to Loved Ones

Often, when I see a couple for the first time, one or both of them look desperate over a basic need not getting met. They look angry and hurt, or caved in and sad, or withdrawn and hopeless. Yet when I ask, "Would you be willing to clearly communicate what you need to your spouse?" they stumble to find the right words, and often fail.

They don't know themselves what they need, not clearly enough to put into words. Or they are stopped cold by an underlying belief that they don't deserve to ask for their needs, or have them met. Or they negate their own chances by playing victim, saying snidely, "I need more affection, but you're always too busy for *my* needs; you couldn't care less what I want." Or they sabotage themselves with vagueness: "I need to feel more loved." ("Feeling loved" means such different things to different people that, unless we paint a specific, clear picture, our partner is left groping in the dark to fill the request.)

We are rarely taught *how* to identify our basic needs clearly. We have to make the effort, as adults, to discover our own needs for touch, contact, affection, sex, joy, and feeling heard. We have to develop a deep trust, in our bones, that we *deserve* to have our basic needs met in a relationship. And we need to learn how to communicate our basic needs clearly, specifically, and directly. In the process, we take full responsibility for giving our needs the highest possible chance of being met.

This requires digging through past rejections, broken trust, and betrayals in order to fully presence our needs. Otherwise, we stay frozen, withholding feelings, withdrawing love, building resentment, and denying our needs. We abandon our needs. We give up, and we project all blame for our unmet needs onto the other person. This is the stuff that leads to affairs, breakups, and couples occupying opposite corners of the same house.

Tom and Marilyn fit this scenario perfectly. Tom had recently found himself attracted to other women. Marilyn had given up on getting her needs met years ago. I spent a few sessions teaching them how to communicate needs clearly. "Drop all the baggage. Start this relationship brand-new," I implored. "Whatever you've convinced yourself you can't get from the other person, toss it. And toss all blaming with it. No licking your wounds. No fantasizing how someday, someone might understand me. All the power to create the relationship you want is in this moment, standing right in front of you. Let's begin."

Marilyn felt the first glimmer of hope. "I need to feel cared about," she told Tom.

"Good, Marilyn," I jumped in, "now tell Tom *as specifically as possible* what feeling cared about looks like and feels like to you. It's different for each person. You sabotage your needs if you expect Tom to know this without telling him. Do you want him to bring you coffee in the morning, or ask you what you are feeling twice a day and *really* listen, or bring you flowers once a week? What is feeling cared about to you?"

She grinned at me like I was Santa Claus, turning every day into Christmas. She said, "Wow! I'm not used to claiming my needs. I usually don't feel like I deserve them.

"I'd love it if you brought me flowers on Friday," she giggled. "But most of all, I need you to care about *me*, not just what I do for you. Ask me how I'm feeling every day. Ask me what I want, in my heart, and then take time to really listen."

Tom nodded and agreed. But Marilyn didn't trust him. "I've heard that before, Tom," she said, "but I'm afraid you won't remember. I'll just get disappointed again."

"Remember, Marilyn," I intervened. "Bottom line, you are responsible for honoring your needs, even when Tom isn't. If he forgets, or he falls back into his unconscious pattern, your responsibility is to state your needs again, louder and clearer, until he responds. Tell him your *whole* truth, which is what you need *and* how you feel when he breaks his promises *and* which fears come up in you when you entertain the idea of speaking your needs. I recommend to all couples that they say their needs to each other at least fifty times before considering giving up."

They both laughed. Later, Tom shared the feelings that lay underneath his desire for an affair.

Taking responsibility is a new, refreshing, empowering way of relating to life, and to ourselves. It is one shortcut to joy. It cultivates inner freedom and compassion. First and foremost, being responsible is coming to terms with our buried needs, with truly loving ourselves. That's the only way to teach loved ones about who we are.

When a client says, "I'm happy," I say, "Good. Now close your eyes and notice how 'happy' feels in your body. Describe it to me. Get real familiar with this, because this is your natural state, your basic goodness. Teach me how you touched the pure essential joy of Being in your core. What choices did you make to allow happiness to shine through? What judgments or doubts did you ignore? What beliefs did you not buy into? What feelings did you face directly and hold in compassion?

Expand this feeling of happiness to fill your whole body." Which path will you choose today?

Practice Tools:

1. Play with taking responsibility. Set an intention each morning to take full responsibility for your reactions. Whenever you feel confused, angry, jealous, or hopeless, ask yourself, "What is *my* part in creating this? How did I react to the situation, and to my feeling about it? How am I suffering by my reaction?" Write down your truth and what you learned from it.

2. Take responsibility for how much joy you are feeling, or not feeling, right now. No matter what is happening around you, whenever you think of it, say, "I choose joy." Witness your feelings, your habitual reaction to this particular feeling, and see it all with a nonjudgmental curiosity. From your expanded Being Self, ask, "How am I stealing my joy away right now?" Stay open to any answers that arise.

3. Practice teaching others what you need. Give yourself lots of room for mistakes as you acquire this new skill. Be as specific, direct, and clear as you possibly can. Keep trying to be more and more specific. When you say, "I need to feel loved," be sure to add, "What helps me feel loved is when you genuinely take time to listen, without interrupting, and then reflect back to me what you heard me say. Or when you look into my eyes, hold my hands, and ask me what I want." Be bold and daring. Act entitled, as if you deserve to have your needs met, which, of course, you do.

"I Don't Deserve Love"

One of the hardest things about
learning to love yourself is to remember that
all you have to do is love yourself
for how you are feeling at the moment.

—GAY HENDRICKS

It's a wild, stormy day in late December. Southwest Colorado is living up to its reputation of changeable weather today, with thick snow coming down one minute, and bright sunshine the next. The weather fluctuates as wildly as our self-worth seems to on those rocky occasions when we're not having the experience we wanted. One young man described this experience to me: "I felt unstoppable for two years, with the most beautiful girl on campus on my arm," he boasted. "But since she left, I can't shake this depression."

This up-and-down phenomenon keeps occurring until we take full possession of our self-worth. As infants, we arrived as brand-new Beings full of love. We loved our parents so unconditionally that, when we saw their pain and wounding, we unconsciously made a pact with them: "I'll do whatever I can," we agreed, "to heal your pain and love you." We learned to attach our self-worth to their approval. If we did what Mom and Dad wanted, we won their praise, approval, and acceptance. But if our actions drew disapproval, we were blamed, shamed, spanked, and sent to our room. Some parents even withdrew love.

When we were unable to heal their wounding and maintain unconditional love, we began to feel unworthy. We blamed ourselves, as children tend to do, and started to believe that something was wrong with us, inside. We rejected the unacceptable places inside us that drew shame, in order to feel loved, even if that love was conditional.

We falsely equated our self-worth with our humanness, or lack of perfection. With no firm boundaries yet, we merged with our parents' negative wounding. When they were incapable of reflecting our true value to us, we concluded we weren't worthy of unconditional love. When our parents judged and criticized *us* rather than just our actions, it fed our sense of unworthiness. We blamed ourselves for it all, as children tend to do.

As adults, most of us still move through the world hoping someone *out there* will prove us worthy. We wander through our lives and ask, "Am I worthy? If I do this to earn your approval, if I hide this rejected part of me, will you find me deserving of love?" At five or ten, we lacked the capacity to protect our self-worth from other people's judgments and prejudices. But now, as adults, we can create new beliefs based on who we truly are. We can give ourselves the unconditional love our parents never could.

The truth is, we are all born worthy and deserving of love. We spend our entire lives basking in unconditional love, whether we know it consciously or not. And we all die worthy of unconditional love. In our essential Being Selves, love is not something we earn, nor something anyone else can take away. It's our natural birthright. Our value doesn't disappear or shrink just because we made a mistake or disappointed someone, or because someone else is angry with us. It's constant, like the sun, like inner joy.

So why are we so scared to let someone truly see who we are deep inside? Why are we so afraid that, if we look inside, we'll find a big empty hole in our center?

Stop Giving Others the Power to Decide Your Self-Worth

It's hard to live in joy if we don't feel worthy. And it's hard to feel truly know-it-in-my-bones, nobody-can-take-it-away worthy if we keep asking somebody else to declare us lovable. Yet that is what we do, far too often. When I work with couples, one person is invariably hurt because the other person keeps failing to deem him or her lovable. An impossible task. We want our lover, spouse, children, best friend, or even a one-night stand to deem us worthy and lovable. But developing self-worth is truly an inside job.

Our Inner Self waits patiently inside for *us*, not somebody else, to tell us we deserve love. My Inner Self waits inside *for me* to love myself, even when I feel sad, even when somebody is angry with me, even when life as I've known it appears to be falling apart all around me. Only we have the power to deem ourselves worthy, deserving of love. Only we can stop giving that power away. Once that power is in place, then our task becomes teaching loved ones how valuable and worthy we are.

For example, Sharon gave her self-worth away for the first twenty years of her adult life. She gave it to her first husband, her second husband, and her last boyfriend. All three left. She was terrified to be herself around them, terrified they would disapprove of her, as her father did. So she stayed busy pleasing others, and hiding her real self. When the third one left, she was devastated, scared her belief was right—that she really was unlovable.

In therapy, I asked Sharon to exaggerate her fear of abandonment. She stood in front of an empty chair, pretending it was her latest lover, and begged, "Please don't leave me. Please, please, please, I'll do anything, just don't leave me." By this point, she had stuck her finger down her throat, signaling that the whole scenario made her gag.

Then I switched places with her. "I'll be your fear," I offered, "and you witness me. Feel free to blurt out whatever words come to you." I moved from one large pillow to the next, treating each as her imaginary lover. "Will you find me lovable, or you, or you?" I pleaded. "If I admire you and never confront you, will you declare me worthy? Deserving of love? And will you do it several times a day, because I keep forgetting?" By now, Sharon was bent over laughing. Then I walked up to her to look her in the eye and imitate her pettern.

"How about you?" I pleaded. "Will you tell me I'm worthy and deserving of love? Please, please?" She shook her head. "Oh my God," she said. "This whole time I've been pressuring men to give me what only I can give myself. Sure, they can love me. And they did. But as long as I'm not worthy in my own eyes, I'll keep pushing them away."

Beliefs love to prove themselves right at our expense. But they can be changed easily once we name the old belief. As Sharon saw that she had been telling her Inner Self, "I don't deserve love," she changed her inner dialogue. She agreed to whisper to her Inner Self every morning, "I'm deserving of unconditional love." She also taught her new lover to help her recognize her old belief so she wouldn't keep pushing him away. Though it didn't save her last marriage, she did change her life, and her sense of self-worth, forever.

Loving Every Aspect Frees Us to Create New Beliefs

All aspects of ourselves need to feel loved, not just the bright, attractive, strong, successful parts, which easily gain approval. In our culture, however, feelings of unworthiness have reached epidemic proportions. The dark shame we feel about being molested needs the light of love shone on it. The guilt we carry over being divorced, having an abortion or affair, or failing in our business venture needs love. The fear we feel about someone finding us boring or empty inside needs love. Any aspect of ourselves we think we have to hide from others needs love, our love. The most common place these rejected aspects look for love is in a safe, supportive, committed relationship.

When someone stands in front of us, saying, "I love you," and really means it, the rejected places inside need to test that love. We rarely test it during the first few months, the "honeymoon phase." But as time passes and it sinks in that this person isn't leaving, those rejected, shameful parts hiding deep inside begin to surface. They rear their ugly heads, expecting to be rejected again (secretly hoping to be loved). They have to know, "Will you still love me now, if I'm screaming angry? Or sad and depressed for days and weeks on end? Or out of control mad with jealousy? Can you still love me *now*?"

Couples often feel surprised when these shadow areas from the past surface in the relationship. "Everything was going so well between us," they say, "I don't understand why he or she had to bring this up now." It's rarely a conscious choice to bring up these unloved parts. It's simply our guilt, fear, shame, or grief grabbing its first opportunity to get what it needed all along: unconditional love. Once it surfaces and is recognized, we can love even this.

An energetic shift occurs when we create a new belief to replace the old one.

Self-Nurturance Helps Us Feel Worthy and Loved

It's one thing to tell ourselves, "I'm worthy and deserving." It's another thing to *feel* worthy and deserving of unconditional love. We have to give ourselves unconditional love first. Then we can receive it from others. We need to listen to *all* of our feelings, and practice self-nurturance, self-appreciation, and self-honoring. It's through these daily acts of kindness toward ourselves that we begin to feel worthy and deserving of love. Through our actions, we teach others how to honor and love us unconditionally.

As we connect with our mature Being Self, and respond with compassion, it becomes much easier to love our shame, our fear, our doubts, and our self-judgments. From this generous post, we begin to develop a healthy, accepting relationship with our Inner Self. We might start by asking our Inner Self each morning, "What are you feeling? What do you need today, based on what you just experienced?" Feeling loved is taking a moment to ask inside, "What belief is fueling this loneliness, fear, or sadness?" It's honoring our feelings directly without getting lost in the story. It's setting time aside each morning for our soul to dance, sing, draw, paint, express itself. It's pausing to love ourselves several times a day by saying, "I love myself for feeling unworthy. I love myself for feeling sad, and for not wanting to feel sad. I love myself for hiding my shame from others, and I love myself for believing I have to hide my shame from others."

If all parts of ourselves deserve unconditional love, then there are no more places left to hide. We get to be who we are, our essential Being, and trust that. When our spirit asks (which it frequently does), "Am I safe to be *me* in the world?" we can answer, "Yes! Yes! Yes!" As we sweep away the old beliefs, our basic goodness emerges. Deep inside, we not only deserve love. We are love. We not only deserve joy. We are joy.

Practice Tools:

1. Become familiar with your old beliefs. Be curious and open as you invite buried beliefs into your awareness. Wonder to yourself, "What belief is fueling my repeated experience of rejection?" Or, "What belief about myself, or the world, is triggering my depression?" Ask sincerely, take some deep breaths, and listen patiently for whatever words or images bubble up into your awareness. Notice what triggers this old belief, and which feelings it triggers. As you recognize the subtle (and not-so-subtle) forms of "I'm unworthy and undeserving" inside, practice naming them out loud and letting them go.

2. Creating new beliefs often brings out a childlike giddiness in us. The minute you identify an old unconscious belief, look in the mirror and state your new belief out loud. State it as a fact, not merely an intention. For instance, rather than, "I am willing to deserve love," say it as if it's already true: "I deserve love. I love myself unconditionally. I receive unconditional love from others." Especially if you uncover shame, guilt, or deep-seated fear, love that place daily.

3. Practice nurturing, honoring, and appreciating yourself. Tell yourself every day, "I love and approve of myself. Life supports and loves me." Notice how it feels in your body to hear this. Check in each morning and ask, "What am I feeling? What does my Inner Self need, based on what I just experienced?" Grow skilled at asking questions and patiently waiting for answers. Create time each day to honor your inner needs, feelings, and heartfelt longings.

4. Remember: unconditional love is something you are born with. Practice telling yourself, "I love myself unconditionally, even when

someone is angry with me, or disappointed in me, or leaves me."
Let loving yourself unconditionally be the secret talisman you carry
in your pocket all the time, no matter what is happening around
you, and no matter what you are feeling inside.

"I'm Afraid to Trust Life"

Authentic joy is not a euphoric state
or a feeling of being high. Rather,
it is a state of appreciation that allows us
to participate fully in our lives.
—PEMA CHODRON

I woke up to six inches of snow Friday morning. It snowed all day Friday, Friday night, and Saturday. By Saturday afternoon, I measured seventeen inches on the deck. The auger cable broke on the snowblower Friday morning, with eight fresh inches already in the driveway. I had to borrow a neighbor's snowblower to clear it.

Saturday morning, I borrowed the same neighbor's Ford pickup to drive the snowblower to the repair shop. On one level, I felt overwhelmed and frustrated. But on another level, on the deep Being level, I knew I was having the experience I was supposed to be having. I trusted what was true. Life is so much like the weather, unpredictable and out of our control. We choose which voice inside ourselves to listen to.

Two voices are always speaking to us, inside, simultaneously. The problem is, we've been trained to listen to our young ego self, the voice of fear. The voice of fear is loud and demanding. It's desperate and pushy. In its panic and anxiety, it badgers us to stay on track, stay on time, stay on top of things, and stay in control. It judges, criticizes, doubts, and fears life, all in the name of keeping us safe and avoiding the "unknown." In a million different versions, it manufactures high drama out of every little thing. And when we're caught up in that drama, we can't hear the soft-spoken, unassuming voice of our Being Self inside. We stifle our joy.

Our wise, mature Being Self is constantly whispering wisdom into our inner ear. It reminds us, moment to moment, that we are always safe, and that we are powerful cocreators with the Universe. In a calm, loving voice, it reassures us that we can handle everything on our plate today, no matter how overwhelming it feels. Whether we listen or not, it's always available to comfort our Inner Self when it's afraid.

At the same time, this loving voice of our Being Self is never pushy, desperate, or demanding. It won't compete with our thoughts or feelings for our attention. It's not even attached to whether we heed its wisdom or not. It simply offers. That's why it's so important that we learn how to pay attention to it. And that we really *hear* the deep inner silence that inevitably comes, after we label our thoughts, "thinking, thinking" or, "fearing, fearing." Only in that silence can we hear the loving wisdom of our hearts.

Looking Inside to Cultivate Deep Inner Trust

The trouble is, most of us are afraid to trust life. If anything, we have learned to mistrust it. And to mistrust ourselves. We were talked out of trusting our intuition by being called stupid, by being told to listen without speaking, or to stop feeling what we were feeling. Now, the minute we feel as if we can't handle what's happening, we instantly revert to those deeply ingrained lessons from childhood. We grab on tight. We take charge, or try to. We manipulate situations to get what we want, and keep getting what we want. We think we can use our personal will to outsmart life before it outsmarts us. But all these are desperate measures from our ego. And usually ineffective in the end.

If we are willing to wake up, these moments of feeling overwhelmed are the perfect time to see our unconscious reactions clearly. As Tarthang Tulku Rinpoche wrote in *Gesture of Balance*, "One of the best ways to discipline our egos is to make friends with ourselves. When we are joyful, the ego becomes calm and does not stir up frustration and discontent . . . Conflict occurs when we do not obey our own inner voice."

This shift from outer to inner trust is well demonstrated by my client Carol. Carol spent the first fifty-one years of her life trusting everyone. In fact, she was so preoccupied with whether people might reject her that she never questioned whether she could trust them. Her "trust barometer" had been broken years ago, when her stepfather molested her. When she told her mother, her mother accused Carol of seducing her stepfather. Carol was shamed into silence, unable to trust anyone, most of all herself. She felt lost.

She escaped her parents by marrying young. However, her first husband abused her, then ran off with another woman. Lovers used her and discarded her. But when her best friend at work betrayed her, she finally realized she needed to learn about trust.

For two whole years, Carol and Susan had commiserated during their lunch hours about how dysfunctional their workplace was. They laughed at how inept and cowardly their boss was. Both secretly agreed to leave within a year. But the day Carol turned in her resignation, Susan was offered Carol's old job, and accepted it. Carol was furious.

"I don't know who to trust, how to trust, or what trust even feels like!" she told me. "I was betrayed by my parents. Everyone close to me has hurt me the most. My husband appears to be a good man, but hell, I don't even trust my own judgment."

I encouraged her to drop down into her body and feel which feeling lived underneath her mistrust. She cried for a long time. Afterwards, I spoke about trust. "The ability to trust was trained out of most of us as young children, so your job now is to reclaim it," I explained. "Trust is receiving. Receiving love, receiving life, receiving the gifts of this moment, whether you like them or not. But if you never received unconditional love as a child, if you were talked out of your feelings and betrayed by the very people who were supposed to protect you, then your trust is deeply broken. We make the mistake of looking *outside* for somebody—a parent, lover, or friend—to trust, when we need to look inside, and learn to trust ourselves." Carol listened intently.

"Buddha gave us the real skinny on trust 2,500 years ago," I continued. "He said the only thing we can truly count on in life is change. Everything is impermanent, he taught, even our own bodies. So trust comes from knowing ourselves, and life, very well.

"In my own life experience, and with clients, I have discovered that inner trust is strengthened by meeting life directly. It comes from being open to what is, whether we like this particular experience or not. From sinking down and meeting every feeling and every fear as it arises. As we do this, we slowly, gradually realize that we can handle it all: Loneliness. Despair. Hopelessness. Rage. Grief. Love. We can handle all of it. Our wise, mature Being Self surrounds all of it with love and compassion. Inner trust builds from being open to our grief and our joy. Each time we dive into whatever feelings we've been avoiding (sometimes for years), we reconnect with our pure joy of Being."

Carol looked mesmerized, as if she had been waiting her whole life to hear this.

"Once broken, trust is very slow to heal. But as we meet each new feeling without resistance, it slowly rebuilds. It builds from hearing the truth in our bellies and our hearts, and trusting it. You see, your inner wisdom, and your inner joy, are always there. They've been there all along. You just have to stop doubting yours, step out of the way."

I asked Carol to close her eyes and take some deep breaths in her belly. As she did this, she located a tightness in her belly. Tears came. "I'm afraid of life," she revealed. "I feel so lost because I don't trust myself or the people around me. When I ask inside where to put my work energy next, I just feel empty and hopeless."

Carol faced her hopelessness by focusing her attention directly on it. She breathed right into the tightness in her belly. Deep grief flowed for several moments. She touched the emptiness and pain she had been avoiding for years. As it subsided, she said, "I feel lighter, more at peace inside. I feel a small ray of hope that I might learn to trust myself."

At home, she practiced asking her Inner Self several times a day, "What am I feeling? What do I need?" After several weeks, her hopelessness reappeared one night. But this time, rather than buying into it and lashing out at her husband, she explained to him how she experienced it inside. She described how the hopelessness felt, what it looked like from her inner eye, and what feelings came with it. He held her for a long time and spoke reassuring words. "I swear, Carolyn," she said, "as soon as he comforted me the way I needed to be comforted as a child, that hopelessness couldn't hang around."

Over the next several months, she faced two job rejections, loss of income, and cancer. The hopelessness was triggered frequently by these events, but slowly she learned to stop dreading it. Instead, she witnessed it and even learned to say, "I love myself for feeling hopeless, and for not wanting to feel hopeless."

She dedicated her days to reclaiming her trust. Each day, she asked her Inner Self, "What am I feeling? What do I need?" She recalled how loving, supportive, and patient she had been with her own daughter, and tried to give herself that same kindness and patience. Rather than compulsively pushing herself to find work (her old pattern), some afternoons she curled up on the couch with a good book. Or napped. Slowly, she came to know trust through loving herself, and listening to the soft, quiet voice inside.

Trading In Manipulation for a Solid Sense of Trust

Our old survival patterns die hard. When push comes to shove, we automatically fall back into survival mode—control and manipulate to get our way—without recognizing what just happened. We try desperately to control the uncontrollable. When conflict strikes at home, or we feel threatened at work, these new, well-meaning tools of consciousness rarely cross our mind. Somehow, when our young ego self is threatened, making an "I" statement about our feelings with the very loved one who is not being there for us, just doesn't seem enough.

Without even thinking about it, we are five years old again, believing the person closest to us is not understanding us. Since it's so hard to catch ourselves in this time warp, it's a perfect time for a loving partner, good friend, or trusted therapist to gently nudge us awake with some loving words of clarity.

Shifting Loyalties to Our Inner Trust

Few of us have the awareness to recognize when our trust barometers are broken. We tend to stay loyal to our basic fear of life, a fear we absorbed into our cells early on, and we tend to stay loyal to that fear until someone, or something, wakes us up. When we say yes to this deeply ingrained fear, and witness the way it manifests in our lives, we free ourselves to respond to the fear with compassion from our mature Being Self.

For instance, Terri arrived in my office extremely frustrated. "I've read every spiritual book on the market," she said. "I worked so hard to reject the same fear of life that consumed my mother. I raised two happy, healthy children with all the unconditional love I could. I meditate twice a day. But no matter how hard I try, I can't make a living at teaching communication to couples. I keep feeling held back by some invisible force." I asked if she was willing to face this "invisible force" directly. She agreed. I set two pillows on opposite ends of the room. "This pillow on your left represents your invisible force," I explained, "and the pillow on your right is your dream job. You are a powerful creator, so show me how you create this dynamic in your life."

She held her right elbow in her left hand as her left arm folded across her diaphragm. Her right arm pointed straight up, cupping her chin in her right hand. "Hmmm," she pondered. "I'm not so good at this drama stuff." Then she stood between the two pillows, facing her dream. "It's like this. I take a step or two toward creating my business, and suddenly I feel pulled backward by some invisible fear. It's an old fear of life that I don't even believe in, but still it has a hold on me. It's as if I'm still loyal to my mother's fear and judgment, even though she's been dead for ten years."

"Good," I said. "Now locate this fear of life in your own body. Turn and face it directly."

She closed her eyes and took some deep breaths. "Right here," she said, reaching behind to brush her back lightly with her right hand. "Right here in my lower back. Which is where I have chronic back pain." I had her lie down to breathe into the fear and release it more fully.

As she breathed directly into the fear lodged in her back, her whole body shook, as if a chill were running through her body. She continued to breathe directly into it, and her legs and torso vibrated until the deep-seated fear was released. "Interesting," she mumbled, "my back feels much more relaxed, much lighter."

She called a week later. "I just had to tell you, Carolyn, that I got four new couple referrals this week, before I even printed my new brochure." When our energy shifts on the inside, the Universe responds to the shift on the outside. When we witness our fear of life directly, consciously, the Universe responds. We always have the choice: to stay unconscious and create what we most fear, or to consciously stay present and create what we want.

As we spend time each day asking our Inner Selves, "What are you feeling and what do you need?" our childlike Inner Self slowly begins to trust us. As we listen to our inner wisdom, we come to trust our intuition. Trust our heart. Trust our feelings and longings. Trust what spirit is trying to tell us through our body symptoms. As we trust ourselves more, we come to trust the experience life is giving us in this moment, even if it makes us uncomfortable. Slowly, gradually, we relax and let go into the present. We open and receive what is. This is trust in its highest form. This newfound inner trust allows us to rest in our pure joy of Being.

Practice Tools:

1. Each morning, whisper to yourself, "I'm willing to trust myself today." Adopt an open, curious attitude about fear, and trust, and life. Ask your Inner Self several times a day, "What am I feeling?" and, "What do I need?" Take deep breaths and patiently listen for the answers. Ask patiently, even if you hear no response the first few times. Many times our Inner Self has felt so hurt and abandoned for so many years that it doesn't trust anyone, including us, with its vulnerable feelings. Treat your Inner Self as a shy young child who needs to be gently coaxed out to play.

2. Take a week to see any ways you block vulnerable feelings, longings, and needs. Set an intention each morning, such as, "I'm willing to notice all the ways I block my vulnerable feelings and needs." Write your discoveries down in large letters on a big piece of paper. Post them on your refrigerator or bathroom mirror—someplace visible where you will bump into them often. Keep a light, humorous attitude, with plenty of permission to make mistakes or look silly.

3. Set aside a half hour. Find a quiet place where you won't be interrupted. Close your eyes, take several deep breaths to relax, and focus on your heart. Ask your heart, "When do I experience my fear of life? How does it stop me from trusting myself and life?" Ask, continue to take deep breaths, and patiently listen for your heart to respond.

4. Another way to welcome this inner wisdom into your awareness is by posing questions inside, such as, "How do I mistrust people? Do I fear the rug being pulled out, or am I constantly waiting for the other shoe to drop? Do I trust, or mistrust, my own intuitions?" (These can even be asked while walking down the street or driving to work.) Listen patiently for your heart's wisdom to respond. When you identify a deep-set fear of life, respond in a brand new way. Let your wise Being Self witness it by offering loving words of reassurance and compassion—the same way you might reassure a young child scared of a nightmare.

5

Jump Starts

Once you have truly embraced God, once you
have made that divine connection, you
will never want to lose it, for it will bring you the
greatest joy you ever had.

—NEALE DONALD WALSCH

WELCOME TO THE FINAL SECTION. IF YOU HAVE BEEN GETTING
to know yourself, making your old habits conscious, and saying yes to
your feelings, thoughts, and beliefs, this section will feel like a breath
of fresh air. Jump Starts offer you a "quickie": a quick way to jump into
joy in seconds. When you don't even have five minutes to exaggerate a
fear, or twenty minutes to lie down, breathe deeply, and connect with
your Being Self, just whisper one of these Jump Starts under your
breath anytime, anywhere, and you will feel your Being expanding into
joy in a matter of seconds.

But don't cheat! These work best *after* you have fully integrated the
three steps into your life by getting to know your feeling habits, mind
habits, and belief habits over time. They work best *after* you have spent
quality time making friends with your Inner Self, cultivating awareness, compassion, and kindness toward yourself. Once you have had
this *body experience* of expanding into inner joy by practicing the steps
day in and day out, no matter what is on your plate, then the Jump
Starts instantly remind you Who You Are in your essential core. It takes
ongoing practice to connect with your wise Being Self and respond
consciously, with compassion, to your humanness every day.

Nobody can love you more, or spend more time with you in this
lifetime, than you. May you become skilled at listening to your Inner
Self, honoring your feelings, respecting heartfelt longings, and holding
all of life's experiences in the loving compassion of your Essence or
Being Self. Enjoy the process!

Setting an Intention

Too often, we believe behavioral changes take a long time—or that we can't change ourselves or anyone else, and just have to live with the behavior. Since we believe this, we block the changes we most want at the starting gate. As you read in the last section, you can create powerful new beliefs in a few seconds. How? By *stating your intentions*.

An intention is one simple, clear sentence about how you want things to be. For instance, if doubt and fear stymie your creativity, your intention might be, "I am free of doubt and fear." Your mind will quickly remind you that it's not true, but just keep stating your intention every morning, and trusting, then watch it become true. By stating your intention out loud, you aim your conscious and unconscious in the direction you want to move.

This empowering move takes only three simple steps:

1. Identify a limiting belief or behavior. This can be done by naming an issue troubling you and taking a moment to be quiet, close your eyes, and ask your heart, "How am I blocking myself from getting what I need?" Ask, take deep breaths, let your mind be blank, and listen for a word, image, or phrase to pop into your intuition. If you don't "hear" anything, be patient.

2. State clearly what you are willing to create for yourself. If you want to feel that your partner is listening to your feelings, say, "I take responsibility for creating a safe, sacred space for my feelings to be heard in my relationship." Cocreate what you want with the Universe. Conscious intentions stop your unconscious from creating what you most fear.

3. State your intention as a fact. Rather than, "I want . . ." as if it might happen at some mysterious future date, say your intention as if it is already true: "My feelings are heard and honored by loved ones." "I am strong and healthy and pain-free." I recommend saying your intention to yourself when you first wake up in the morning.

"Am I Here Now?"

S o often, amidst our busy lives, our bodies and hearts are sur-
rounded by the songs of birds we cannot hear, natural beauty we
cannot see, and day-to-day love we forget to feel. Too often, our souls
are brimming with longings we forget to embody and inner wisdom
we forget to hear. Why? Because our mind has dragged our awareness
off into some memory or plan and captured our attention. But we
are not obligated to stay there.

You are under no obligation to even let your current thought finish
its sentence!

One of the quickest ways to presence yourself, and jump back into
joy, is to ask, "Am I here now?" No matter what thought your mind is
chewing on, or what feeling you are completely consumed by in this
moment, ask yourself, "Am I here now?" It instantly cuts through intense
thoughts and feelings, and brings you into this present moment. How?
It puts space and loving acceptance around whatever you are thinking or feeling. In short, it shifts focus from the story in your head to
the aliveness in this present moment.

If you can't remember, "Am I here now?" just whisper, "yes" when you
inhale and exhale. Do it as many times as you need to, until you feel your
body begin to relax. Whether sitting at your desk, riding the commuter
train, or standing in the grocery line, close your eyes and let "yes" ride
your breath. It melts all resistance (and dissolves whatever fear or worry
was preoccupying your awareness). It brings you fully into the present and helps you know inside, and trust, that you can handle it, no
matter what *it* is.

"I Choose Joy"

We make choices all the time. Mostly unconscious ones, below our awareness. We fall into bitterness over some hurt, and unconsciously design a lifestyle out of it. Or we linger in resentment, closing our hearts off to our lover and the world. Every moment, we relax with what is, or we resist. We enter this world each morning with our hearts open to the ten thousand joys and ten thousand sorrows of life, or we shut down. We trust the experience we are having and face it directly, or we mistrust the invisible wisdom of the Universe. We reassure our soft, vulnerable beings that we are safe and loved for exactly Who We Are, or we buy into fear. Since we make choices all the time anyway, why not choose joy?

Play with having your first thought every morning be: "I choose joy." Set the intention: "Whatever happens today, whether I like it or hate it, whether it's pleasant or uncomfortable, I'm willing to choose joy." Keep saying it until you feel in your bones that this essential joy is filling your awareness to overflowing. If you keep choosing joy and still can't feel it, ask yourself, "How am I stealing my joy away right now?" Ask, take some deep breaths, and listen for your inner wisdom to answer. If someone is yelling at you, or disappointed with you, or doing exactly what you asked him or her not to do, whisper inside, "I choose joy." When you choose joy, it holds your current experience in love by reminding your soft, quiet Inner Self that he or she is loved, and that nobody can take this love away, no matter what.

Once you touch a glimmer of joy inside, try expanding it. Imagine blowing breath and life into it as if blowing up a balloon. With each exhale, picture blowing your breath into the joy feeling, and feel it expand inside. Soon, your entire being is filled with the soft, ever-present feeling of joy. Feel the palpable energy shift. Watch your vision broaden and expand. In this process, you put space around you and whatever you are feeling or experiencing. You have given your Being Self more elbow room to feel itself.

Also, try carrying a small stone or crystal in your pocket or purse. Every time your hand bumps into it, let it be a reminder to tell yourself, "I choose joy." It doesn't matter if you've been consumed by intense frustration, disappointment, or loneliness for two minutes, two days, or two years. The second you remember, say, "I choose joy."

As often as you think of it, even during the most outrageous of circumstances, when you can't conceive of joy sharing this moment with what you are feeling, whisper, "I choose joy" under your breath.

Breathe joy in and out of your heart. Let it ride your breath by saying, "joy" when you inhale and, "joy" when you exhale for several minutes, until you feel inner joy. Or experiment with it by saying, "yes" when you inhale and, "joy" when you exhale. Or saying, "love" when you inhale and, "joy" when you exhale. When you touch fear, or shame, or loneliness, or despair, even then, let joy ride your breath. We are constantly talking to our Inner Selves anyway, so talk to yourself as a great lover or good friend. In this moment, every moment, choose joy.

Give Yourself What You Need

It's pretty tough to access your joy without knowing—let alone giving yourself—what you need. I'm not talking about "needing" money or chocolate or a new car, but about accessing the truth inside your heart. I'm talking about stepping fully into the present moment, dropping the "plan," whatever it is, no matter how necessary it might sound, and genuinely, sincerely asking your heart, "What do I need, based on what I've just been experiencing?" Not in a rushed way, skating right over the answer as your ego convinces you that you must push ahead to meet some imaginary deadline it made up in your head. But respectfully, by asking, "What do I need *now*?" and patiently listening for the answer deep inside. And, of course, trusting the answer.

As you listen for the soft, gentle voice of your Inner Self, you may discover that you need quiet time. Or contact with a close friend. Your body may need to swim today, and feel the refreshing joy of swimming, rather than use the treadmill. Taking a hot bath may sound good, even though you had no clue until a moment ago that that was what you needed. Or drawing, painting, or feeling clay in your hands. Maybe dancing in the living room to loud music. Let yourself hear what your Inner Self longs for. Don't censor.

Too often we look outside ourselves, hoping that loved ones will notice we are upset, or sad, or gloomy, and will ask us what we need. But the truth is, *we* teach loved ones how to honor our needs by how we respect (or don't respect) our own needs. And when we honor our basic needs for exercise, reflection time, contact, sexual and nonsexual touch, and those things that bring us joy, we teach our children how to include their basic human needs in their busy lives, too.

Each morning, before getting out of bed, take five minutes to check in with your Inner Self. Place one hand over your heart, and the other hand over your belly. Close your eyes. Take several deep breaths in your belly, as if breathing deep in your belly is the only thing you have to do all morning. When you feel relaxed, focus your attention on your heart. Gently ask, "What does my Inner Self need today?" or, "What do I need, based on what I'm feeling?" Let go of any thoughts. Just ask, breathe, and listen patiently. If still nothing comes, ask again. Doing this even once a day will get you in the habit of making space for your needs, and feeling that there really is room for your needs.

Asking questions is a soft, gentle way to access your inner wisdom. Another good one is, "What sounds good?" This is different from "planning" to exercise, meditate, or do yoga today. Remember, you want to step into this moment with no agenda at all except to listen to what your Inner Self most needs. If you can't fit it in today, promise your Inner Self that you can fit it in soon—tomorrow, or this weekend.

Whenever you notice yourself feeling impatient, stressed, or irritable during the day, take a few minutes to "check in." Sit or lie down. Close your eyes. Take some deep breaths in your belly until you feel relaxed, then ask inside, "What do I need *now*, based on what I've been experiencing?" Sometimes you may just need to deep breathe for ten minutes to completely shift and rebalance your energy. Other times, you may need to set time aside to journal your feelings, or address an issue with your mate or friend. Don't let the mind jump in with "I don't need anything" or, "I just need some caffeine and I'll be fine." Let your heart answer. And remember to respond with kindness.

State Your Needs Specifically

More than anything, we all hunger to be seen, heard, acknowledged, and understood. Yet this most important step forward begins with ourselves.

In Tantric sex, you are encouraged to tell your lover *exactly* what turns you on, where you like to be touched, how long you like to kiss and pet and practice foreplay, how much pressure you like where and when, and so on. Why? Because this maximizes your chances of being pleasured the way you most want to be, to feel loved.

I want to borrow that concept and encourage you to practice "Tantric love" or "Tantric communication." I don't care what you call it. Just do it. Practice and practice getting more and more specific with loved ones, until you feel, inside, that your needs are being met. Even while manifesting your next vision, tell the Universal Waitress (that sweet, invisible waitress standing above you in a red-checkered apron, notepad in hand, writing down the specific order of your vision) *exactly* what you want. Be as specific as you are when ordering a tall half-caf, half-decaf latte with soy.

Rather than silencing or postponing your needs, state your needs specifically. For more practice, after you feel that you have communicated clearly, state your needs again, even more specifically. Keep honing your skill. Be sure to include your *whole truth*, which includes any fears or feelings you notice arising as you prepare to state your needs.

You vastly increase your chances of getting your needs met by being specific.

If this feels intimidating, set an intention each morning: "I deserve to have my needs met, and I'm willing to state my needs clearly and specifically." Then, when you have a need, instead of saying, "I want to feel more loved," or, "I need to feel included," describe what "feeling more loved" looks like and sounds like to you, personally.

Even when you think you have communicated clearly, practice stating your needs more and more specifically. Say, "I want to feel more loved, and what makes me feel loved is _____ (when you put down the cell phone and listen to my feelings; when you create a spontaneous weekend away for us; when you rub my feet; when you cuddle me in the morning, or initiate lovemaking). It doesn't matter what it is. It matters that you communicate clearly what helps you feel loved.

And when you don't feel heard, practice restating your need (rather than giving up). Say, "I'm not sure you understood me; let me state my need more clearly." Give yourself plenty of permission to sound like a broken record.

Just keep clarifying your needs until they are met. Don't give up. Drop those deadly expectations and past resentments. Forget how many times you've asked before. Don't bother to listen to that old belief that "there's no room for my needs." Remember, every moment, you are always teaching loved ones who you are and what you need.

Appreciate What Is

Where we focus our attention brings us great joy, or our next anxiety attack. It is a moment-to-moment choice we make. Sometimes, we get so caught up in the future, we forget to take pleasure in what we have. We become so obsessed with "I want, I want, I want," there is no room left to notice that we are already standing neck-deep in grace.

Too often, we fret endlessly over the money we haven't made, the current conflict at work, our back pain returning, the children's grades, our upcoming "fun" vacation, or the retirement plan that's not in place. In other words, we focus too much on what we are not getting and not enough on appreciating everything that is going smoothly.

Let's reverse this. Whether you are worried, frustrated, doubting yourself, or just running a story, in this moment, stop it. Press pause in your mind. Shift into spending a few minutes appreciating ten things that you have. It may sound like, "I appreciate my good health, my relationship, my family and friends, my work, all the money and assets I do have, and the love in my life." Appreciate what is going well—for example, that your father's surgery went well, that your knee injury is healing, that your home (though not yet your dream home) is safe and warm, and that you had time to work out today. *Appreciate what is* as often as you think of it.

Take a few moments at the end of each day to appreciate your mate, friends, and children for whatever they did today: Appreciate them for working or going to school, for bringing home groceries, for preparing dinner or washing dishes, for caring for the younger children, for doing their homework or practicing piano, and for being kind to you. Appreciate the simple day-to-day things that we too often take for granted.

"What Is My Part Here?"

Nothing weeds out old beliefs as quickly as self-responsibility. Nothing busts your habit of playing victim, giving up on yourself and your needs, and blaming others, quite like responsibility. Taking responsibility is not about blaming yourself, or making it your fault. It's about empowering yourself to *see your part* clearly and take appropriate action. It cuts to the truth. And it is the short path to inner joy.

The next time you find your mind chewing ravenously on who did what to you, drop the story line and ask yourself, "What is my part here?" The next time you are consumed by anger, fear, or despair, say, "I'm willing to take full responsibility for my feelings here." When your favorite belief has caught you in its web, justifying your actions and making the other person wrong, ask, "What is my part in painting myself into a corner here?" When you are bored with work or your relationship, ask, "How did I let boredom replace my creative energy and my dreams?" When you find yourself unhappy and filled with resentment, ask, "What price am I paying for stealing my joy away now?" However many ways you can say it creatively, keep asking, "What is my part here?"

When you ask, you access your inner wisdom. You engage your intuition and your mature Being Self to bestow its infinite wisdom upon you. Ask, take some deep breaths, ignore ego's pride (which likes to cover up any self-responsibility), and listen patiently for your heart's answer. In other words, whenever it looks as if someone, or something, on the "outside" is causing your pain, open to *your* responsibility. It is one of the most freeing moves you will ever make. But don't take my word for it. Try it and see.

"What Does My Soul Need?"

One Friday afternoon in July, while hiking with a friend, I started giggling like a young schoolgirl. My very being overflowed with joy. I was immersed for hours in wildflowers that only bloom above 10,000 feet a few weeks out of the year. Iridescent pink Parry's primrose cascaded down trickling creeks. Lavender and white columbine clustered on lush green mountainsides. Magenta, pink, and white paintbrush blanketed meadows like a carpet. Bluebells, larkspur, yellow arnica, maroon bells, and purple fringe all stood majestically. And to top off this spectacle, I spent lunchtime watching sixty elk and their babies play on a patch of snow above the tree line. This high-altitude hiking feeds my soul.

We all need to feed our souls. But first, we need to offer our souls a safe container in which to figure out what they need when, knowing that this can change day to day. Today, your soul may want to dance, draw, paint, or sing. Or lie on the floor doing "nothing," drinking in Bach, Mozart, or old Cat Stevens. Get in the habit of asking your soul what it needs.

Of course, asking only takes a few seconds. It's waiting for a response that can take time, even try our patience. Soul often responds so slowly that we start thinking, "Nothing's happening here. I must not be doing it right." Let that impatience go. Just close your eyes, take several deep, relaxing breaths in your belly, and ask again, "What does my soul need?" Ask, deep breathe, and patiently listen for the answer.

Soul may not even bother to answer you at all the first several times you ask. It has to get to know you, feel your sincerity, trust that you do respect its wisdom, and feel that you genuinely do want to create time for it. After all, soul lives in the eternal present, so it has all day, and then some. Soul time is different from any preplanned event.

When you go to the gym, you know you are going to use the treadmill for thirty minutes, do weight training for twenty, and/or swim for half an hour. When you sit down to meditate, you have a specific practice in mind. But soul lives in the timeless present. Money, fame, success, the Dow Jones average, and deadlines matter little to soul.

Awareness, presence, being, connection, love, joy, acceptance, trust—
these are the spaces soul lives in.

Soul moves from one experience to the next, letting feelings and
inner wisdom guide its way. Its focus is constantly giving our Being
Self what it needs to come back into integrity, which can change from
moment to moment. It's so worth it, though. It gives us that sense of
wholeness we all love. As you begin to include soul's needs in your day-
to-day life, you may notice a humming in your heart, as if everything
is going to be all right.

Set aside an hour today, or a day soon, to connect with your soul. Ask
loved ones not to interrupt you. Silence the phone. Find a quiet place
to lie down, close your eyes, and take several deep breaths in your belly,
as if you had the whole rest of the day just to deep breathe. Focus on
your heart center. Imagine breathing in and out of your heart.

Then softly ask your heart, "What does my soul need?" Take deep
breaths and patiently listen for an image, word, or feeling to enter your
awareness. If nothing bubbles up from inside, ask again. Be as patient
and kind as you might be with a young child who was ignored for far
too many years. If still nothing comes, don't get mad or give up. Just try
asking a different way. "What sounds good right now?" "What would
I love to do?" When you do get an answer, promise your soul that you
will set aside an hour each day for "soul time."

Now, keep your promise. After a while, as your body and soul receive
the gift of soul time each day, it will no longer feel like a luxury. It will
soon become a necessity for your Being, a source of inner joy.

A Lifelong Commitment to Joy

Make a lifelong commitment to joy, day by day, moment by moment. Think of this powerful process as slowly peeling away your defensive shell, appreciate the uniqueness and beauty of each layer along the way, not rushing or forcing this tender new process. After all, our hearts, our bodies, our intuition, and our breath all live in the eternal present moment. Every time you realize you have been lost in disappointment, despair, loneliness, or fear (for hours, days, or years), let that be a moment of celebration, remembering to choose joy even now.

Let yourself say yes to what is, especially in those dark times when mind can't fathom joy sharing the same moment with your current distress. Let joy fill you with more inner peace than your limited mind ever thought possible. Let joy become your lucky talisman, walking with you into every new experience, every dark alley, every step into the unknown, so that you never feel alone again.

Let witnessing your feelings, mind habits, and beliefs become your best friend. Let it be the new pair of spectacles you wear into each new moment, allowing you to see life, and yourself, from your mature Being Self in ways you never imagined. Let witnessing take you by the hand and lead you into the creative endeavors and deep intimacy of your wildest dreams.

Let responding with compassion be your new mantra. Respond to your own fear, doubt, judgment, and shame with the same open heart and loving compassion you would show a young child. For trusting your inner wisdom is your pot of gold at the end of the rainbow. Live from your heart in the eternal now, where all the power is. Relax with what is. Trust your deep heart wisdom.

Selected Bibliography

Almaas, A. H. *Diamond Heart, Book Four*. Berkeley, CA: Diamond Books, 1997.

———. *Essence*. York Beach, ME: Samuel Weiser, 1986.

———. *The Pearl Beyond Price*. Berkeley, CA: Diamond Books, 1988.

Chodron, Pema. *The Places That Scare You*. Boston, MA: Shambhala, 2001.

———. *Start Where You Are*. Boston, MA: Shambhala, 1994.

———. *When Things Fall Apart*. Boston, MA: Shambhala, 1997.

Choquette, Sonia. *Your Heart's Desire*. New York: Three Rivers, 1997.

Friedman, Lenore, and Susan Moon. *Being Bodies*. Boston, MA: Shambhala, 1997.

Hendricks, Gay. *Learning to Love Yourself*. New York: Prentice Hall Press, 1987.

Hendricks, Gay, and Kathlyn Hendricks. *At the Speed of Life*. New York: Bantam Books, 1993.

———. *The Conscious Heart*. New York: Bantam Books, 1997.

———. *Conscious Loving*. New York: Bantam Books, 1990.

His Holiness the Dalai Lama, and Nickolas Vreeland. *An Open Heart*. Boston, MA: Little, Brown and Company, 2001.

Kornfield, Jack. *After the Ecstasy, the Laundry*. New York: Bantam Books, 2000.

———. *A Path with Heart*. New York: Bantam Books, 1993.

Lowen, Alexander. *Bioenergetics*. New York: Penguin Books, 1975.

———. *The Language of the Body*. New York: Collier Books, 1971.

Mindell, Arnold. *Working with the Dreaming Body*. New York: Viking Penguin, 1985.

Mindell, Arnold, and Amy Mindell. *Riding the Horse Backwards*. New York: Penguin Books, 1992.

Pierrakos, John C. *Core Energetics*. Mendocino, CA: LifeRhythm Publications, 1987.

Poonja, H. W. L. *Wake Up and Roar*. Kula, HI: Pacific Center Publishing, 1992.

————. *Wake Up and Roar, Vol. 2*. Kula, HI: Pacific Center Publishing, 1993.

Rodegast, Pat, and Judith Stanton. *Emmanuel's Book II: The Choice for Love*. New York: Bantam Books, 1989.

————. *Emmanuel's Book III: What Is an Angel Doing Here?* New York: Bantam Books, 1994.

Sewell, Marilyn. *Cries of the Spirit*. Boston, MA: Beacon Press, 1991.

Tulku, Tarthang. *Gesture of Balance*. Berkeley, CA: Dharma Publishing, 1977.

————. *Hidden Mind of Freedom*. Berkeley, CA: Dharma Publishing, 1981.

————. *Kum Nye Relaxation, Parts I & II*. Berkeley, CA: Dharma Publishing, 1978.

————. *Skillful Means*. Berkeley, CA: Dharma Publishing, 1978.

Williams, Terry Tempest. *An Unspoken Hunger*. New York: Pantheon Books, 1994.

Woodman, Marion. *Conscious Femininity*. Toronto: Inner City Books, 1993.

————. *The Pregnant Virgin*. Toronto: Inner City Books, 1985.

Woodman, Marion with Kate Danson, Mary Hamilton, and Rita Greer Allen. *Leaving My Father's House*. Boston, MA: Shambhala, 1992.

Woodman, Marion, and Elinor Dickson. *Dancing in the Flames*. Boston, MA: Shambhala, 1996.

Woodman, Marion, and Jill Mellick. *Coming Home to Myself*. Berkeley, CA: Conari Press, 1998.

About the Author

As therapist, writer, teacher, and workshop leader, Carolyn Hobbs has spent over twenty years teaching clients, couples, and students the path to consciousness and joy. With candid humor, deep insight, and loving compassion, she gently guides people through the thorny bushes of human conditioning into their wise, mature Being Selves.

A licensed marriage and family therapist, Carolyn has a body-centered therapy practice in Durango, Colorado. She has a master's in Humanistic Psychology and has trained intensively with Gay and Kathlyn Hendricks, co-authors of *Conscious Loving, Conscious Heart, Lasting Love,* and *At the Speed of Life*. In addition to teaching psychology classes at Naropa Institute and Ft. Lewis College, she has published articles in *Personal Transformation* magazine and *AHP Perspective*, the international journal of the Association for Humanistic Psychologists. Carolyn has devoted her adult life to the path of consciousness, focusing on meditation, Buddhist studies, bioenergetics, breathwork, and body-centered therapies. She lives in southwest Colorado.

To Our Readers

Conari Press, an imprint of Red Wheel/Weiser, publishes books on topics ranging from spirituality, personal growth, and relationships to women's issues, parenting, and social issues. Our mission is to publish quality books that will make a difference in people's lives—how we feel about ourselves and how we relate to one another. We value integrity, compassion, and receptivity, both in the books we publish and in the way we do business.

Our readers are our most important resource, and we value your input, suggestions, and ideas about what you would like to see published. Please feel free to contact us, to request our latest book catalog, or to be added to our mailing list.

Conari Press
An imprint of Red Wheel/Weiser, LLC
P.O. Box 612
York Beach, ME 03910-0612
www.conari.com